GLORY GONE

The story of nailing in Bromsgrove

First published in Great Britain in 1989 by
Halfshire Books
5 The Green Cutnall Green Worcestershire WR9 0PW

Reprinted with revisions 1999

ISBN 1899062 04 1

Printed and bound in Great Britain by printinblack,
Midsomer Norton, Bath

GLORY GONE

The story of nailing in Bromsgrove

Bill Kings and Margaret Cooper

 Halfshire Books

Contents

Acknowledgments

To our spice

Preface

As a young child of three or four I formed a vivid impression of my grandfather's nailshop. The door was of two halves, the bottom half latched, the top half open to let in the light and draught. There was one small window with vertical iron bars but no glass. At night the window was shuttered close but even on a sunny day the nailshop was dark and gloomy.

As you stepped into the shop from outside there was a six-inch drop to an earthen floor, packed hard. The smell was the most striking thing and every nailshop smelt the same from the mixture of breeze and scale from the iron as it was hammered, still red hot. The scale flew off the end of the rod onto the floor which, after over a century of use, had become more scale than earth, a hard surface which prevented the erosion of the floor from the millions of times the nailmaker had to turn and walk the couple of steps from the fire to the block. I was to meet up with this same smell later on in life for it occurs in the vicinity of any blacksmith's shop or stamp shop where drop hammers are operating.

Although the nailshop looked untidy there was a set place for everything: the nail iron, the breeze, a spare ash pole. A pair of scales hung on the wall and there was a shelf for the spare bores and inserts for the oliver for different types of nail. Every inch of space was used. Later on I was to discover that even the spare bits of wall were used to hang up orange boxes in which ducks or hens would nest.

What was it like entering the nailshop at four o'clock in the morning, the normal starting time? A single candle, stuck on the frame of the block, was all the light the nailer had to prepare his fire and get out his tools. Even when the fire was going the candle was still necessary as the fire's glow was always hidden by the nailer's body as he turned to make the nail. Once a dozen or so nails had been made the nailer was into his stride, keeping up the rhythm of swinging from fire to block for up to twelve or fourteen hours a day. The monotony and laboriousness of the job was soul-destroying.

But to the onlooker, who stayed to watch for five minutes or so, the rhythm and skill required were fascinating: a couple of puffs at the bellows; the extraction of the rod from the fire and the tap on its end to knock off the scale; a turn and couple of steps from fire to block; a dozen or so deft clouts to form the tang; another deft tap on the hardy to partially sever the nail; the wrench of the iron to tear off the nail as it lay on the bore; the bang on the yod (nail head) with the oliver to give it its final shape; and finally the ejection of the completed nail by a slight tap on the paddle with a 2lb lump hammer.

The whole series of operations took only seconds but woe betide anyone or anything that provided distraction. Hob nails were fetching 4½d per thousand and the nailer had to make three or four thousand daily for the family to exist.

In its heyday there were over three thousand nailers in Bromsgrove alone and the area's history in the eighteenth, nineteenth and early twentieth centuries inevitably centres on the trade. It has grown increasingly urgent to record this history while there are still some living who remember the work of the nailer. This record results from the collaboration of one whose nailing connections are lifelong, the last forty-five years spent investigating and talking about all things nailing, and one who has come fresh to the subject, undertaking further research and editing the material.

The story of the hand-wrought nail trade in the Bromsgrove area is called *Glory Gone,* a phrase used by Charlie Troth of York Road, Sidemoor (that haven of intellectual excellence!). Charlie, a master as well as a maker of nails, was the district's last hand-wrought nailmaker but the words 'glory gone' must have been uttered with some irony. In 1952 the 'New Statesman and Nation' reported his sigh for 'glory gone' but also his additional comment:

> First to last, ours was a sweated trade, little better than clemmin'; we're well done with it.

One   The staple trade

Nails are still part of our everyday conversation. Generation after generation has turned to them for a handy phrase which says all: 'hit the nail on the head', 'get down to brass tacks', 'nail your colours to the mast', 'another nail in the coffin'. Such adages speak of the long-established and indispensable trade of the nailmakers whose products were for centuries the great fixers. Nowadays there are rivals, of course, superglue, gripper rods, interlocking tiles. But though carpet tacks, for instance, may be things of the past, there are still plenty of nails needed and being made.

Not, however, by hand. The wrought-iron nailmaking industry has long died; but for several hundred years it was a vital part of the employment scene, this widespread occupation assuming greatest importance in the West Midlands and becoming eventually Bromsgrove's staple trade.

For thousands of years nails of one sort or another have been made. One of the very first references to iron nails comes in the Bible where (in I Chronicles 22 v3) David began building the temple and 'prepared iron in abundance for the nails for the doors of the gates, and for the joinings'. An earlier incident, when Jael hammered a tent nail into the head of her husband Sisera (Judges 4 v21), may appear to have got the industry off to a bad start — but the nail in question, it must be said, was a wooden peg.

There were however some gruesome incidents in the early history of the iron nail such as that recorded by the nineteenth-century local historian of Bromsgrove, John Cotton, in his long poem 'Nails Old and New'[1] which traces the eventful history of nails:

> I think of the nail with chased scrolling—
> Made finely in gold, bronze and silver—
> Which served classic ladies for hair-pins.

One Fulvia used as a dagger,
When mad with vindictive resentment,
She brutally outraged dead Cicero;
For, the murdered man's head by her orders
Being brought her, she pulled from his still lips
The tongue, and repeatedly stabbed it;
That tongue which had censured her husband
And whose truth her own act gave proof of
Since it said once 'no animal living
Could be so revengeful as woman'.

The Celts had been mining and forging iron for several centuries before the Romans set foot in Britain, skilful metalworkers, able not only to meet the basic needs of their tribal communities—barrel hoops, plough wheels and shares and swords—but also to fashion objects more artistic and ornate. It was once thought the Celts were neither makers of nails nor of horseshoes. But a find of historic interest in Bulbury in Dorset suggests otherwise for among the late Iron Age objects revealed by the excavation were chains, an anchor and some nails, the latter between six and seven inches long.[2]

But the Romans have left abundant evidence all over Europe of their widespread use of nails. In the museum in Saalburg, West Germany, for example, there is a Roman nailblock little different from the ones used in Bromsgrove and other nailmaking districts as late as the middle of the twentieth century. In this country, as elsewhere, nails were in demand in the building of frontier forts, the mushrooming of villas, the growth of towns—nails for roof tiles, nails for fixing wood, from large timbers to small bucket handles. And then there were the soldiers themselves, heavy on footwear since they were expected to march at least 15 miles a day and sometimes twice as far. Like the old British swaddy his boots were well hobbed but, unlike his British counterpart, he was paid *clavarum*, or nail money.

The industrious nature of the Roman nailmaker is plentifully evident and a most interesting discovery of nearly thirty years ago demonstrates his degree of skill. In 83AD a legionary fortress was established at Inchtuthil, near Aberdeen in Scotland, but evacuated four years later. The Romans left in a hurry but not before burying in a twelve-foot pit some 600,000 nails, three of them illustrated over the page.

From hob nail to large timber nail—and everything in between—the iron had to be flattened and chiselled manually into strips. Interestingly, the middle-sized nail, apart from the head being a little worn, is almost identical to a Spanish-made rose-head nail and also to a Bromsgrove rose-head hundreds of years later; and in all three varieties it is possible to count the number of blows required to fashion the tang, or point, of the nail (25/30). Only an engineer can understand the high degree of skill required to shape this tang from metal of about ¼ inch in diameter.

In common with a number of crafts and trades, nailmaking almost

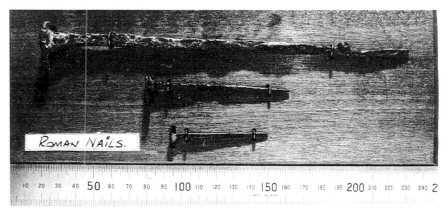

Roman nails from Inchtuthil

certainly declined with the departure of the Romans in the fifth century; but it did not disappear. Little evidence of the nail industry in the middle ages has survived but smiths continued to make the small nails needed for leather footwear, for example, and the larger nails for hinges on castle and church doors; and spikes, the speciality of some ironworkers, were in demand at a time in our history when four-legged spikes were an essential aid in boarding the enemy's ship and driving its crew overboard.

For many hundreds of years nails were made not by nailers but by general blacksmiths along with their own work; and many farmers possessed a small forge where simple iron products including nails could be made. In attempting to find the beginning of the specialist hand-wrought nailmaking industry in the West Midlands, William Hutton argued for the fourteenth century.[3] Some have regarded this as too early a dating but it may not be too far off the mark. The Victoria County History rightly suggests that the making of nails was probably simultaneous with the working of iron ore from the South Staffordshire coalfield and this was established a very long time before the usefulness of coal was discovered in the seventeeth century.[4]

We know for certain that nailmaking as a separate craft from that of the general smith must have been well established by the sixteenth century. John Leland, antiquarian and traveller during the reign of Henry VIII, passed through part of Birmingham in the late 1530s and noted that there were 'many smiths in the towne . . . and a great many naylors' who got their 'yren out of Staffordshire and Warwikeshire and see cole out of Staffordshire'.[5] There is a slightly earlier reference to Worcestershire nails in the 1538 accounts for the building of Nonsuch Palace in Surrey which record that English nails were bought from Reynolde Warde of Dudley, nailman, at 11/4d per thousand.[6] (This was more than twice the price, incidentally, of Flemish nails—so presumably they must have been good!) More locally still, Stourbridge nails were used when Grafton Manor was being built for John Talbot in 1568/69.[7]

By 1584 there was already concern about over-easy entrance into the trade for in that year a bill was drafted to regulate the number of apprentices to be kept by a master and to recognize nailmaking as a separate trade in Worcestershire, Staffordshire and Shropshire: 'No one but those apprenticed and trained to it to practise it, and no apprentice to set up shop as a nailer unless he be 30 years old or married.'[8] And by the early 1600s the trade was so established it had had time to develop some of the disturbing features which were the cause of so many enquiries in the nineteenth century, a situation clearly hinted at in the title of a bill read out in the House of Commons in 1604: 'For Relief of Poor Artificers, called Blacksmiths and Nailors; and for Avoiding of Deceits in their Trades and of Oppression daily practised upon them'.

The West Midlands nail trade then was in full swing by the first half of the sixteenth century and very possibly the century before (though perhaps not quite so early as Hutton has suggested, a little late on the scene presumably for handing down the surname Nailer in anything like the way the much older craftsman Mr Smith has done). The more settled society that resulted from the end of the Wars of the Roses, the rise in population and growing prosperity under the Tudors, the requirements of an expanding navy, the beginnings of international trade, activity on the domestic building front, especially the trend for inserting floorboards—all these developments meant an increase in demand for nails.

In its very early stages nailmaking was undoubtedly carried on in the same way as other crafts with the nailer as his own master, obtaining his own raw materials, making the nails with the help of his family, journeyman and apprentice, perhaps, and selling direct to his customers. But it was always a very scattered operation and it cannot have been long before the ironmonger (ironmaster) appeared, specializing in selling the nails to customers near and far and thus standing between the nailmaker and the consumer.

As Court has pointed out,[9] the West Midlands at the beginning of the seventeenth century, though an important centre of the country's leading industry, cloth, was a rather out-of-the-way area, a long way from the sea and ports and served by poor roads which were little better than bridle paths. Fortunately there was the River Severn, comparatively near and crucial at a time when—until the great road improvements of the later years of the eighteenth century—rivers were more important than roads, vital in promoting trade between one area and another and, by carrying goods to the sea, able to make it international.

Bewdley, on the river, came to play a crucial part in the trade between the West Midlands and the rest of the world. Iron from the Forest of Dean, from Belgium and later from as far afield as Sweden came to Bristol and travelled up the Severn to Bewdley, a key point for this and a great variety of other goods which for so long could travel more cheaply by water. There the great ironmasters kept stock houses. 'As many as four hundred horses could be watered and fed' in the town according to Nash.[10] The few miles from Bewdley to Birmingham and the Black Country were covered by packhorse, a good one able to carry between 2 and 2½cwt in panniers—carts and waggons taking over only after the tracks became turnpike roads.

From its geographical position North Worcestershire was close to supplies of two raw materials, iron and coal, and within easy access of a river which was navigable for most of the year as far as Shrewsbury for larger boats, a river reputed to be the busiest in Europe in the seventeenth century, except for the Meuse. It is not very suprizing therefore that by 1600 Dudley and Stourbridge should have developed as important centres of the iron industry and that nailmaking, the iron industrys's most prolific branch, should be thick on the ground between Dudley in the north and Bromsgrove and Belbroughton in the south.[11]

The Quarter Sessions Rolls for Worcestershire, which cover the period from 1591—1643, demonstrate how widespread nailmaking had become in the north of the county. Of the 54 Dudley men mentioned, for example, 20 were nailers. And it is in these records that we get an early reference to a Bromsgrove nailer, Nicholas Saunders, a 'staff naylor' who appeared in the court on 14 June 1610. There are further references in the rolls to Bromsgrove nailers during this period:

1620	Henry Bradley	indicted for stealing wood from a Mr & Mrs Williams
1625	Edward, William and John Staunton	Edward had picked a fight with Thomas Tyndall, a Bromsgrove labourer
1634	Thomas Waringe and his wife Joan	for keeping the peace towards Jane Batch
	Thomas Tearne	for keeping the peace towards another nailing family
1637	John Turton	prosecuting two vagrant women called Robinson (later Roberson) for stealing his goods. The women claimed to have found them in a bush near his house! 5 months later Anna and Elizabeth were still in gaol
1640	William Founes	for keeping the peace towards Thomas Dudley, a constable of Dudley

The earliest known reference to a Bromsgrove nailer comes from the parish registers of St John the Baptist where an entry on 24 January 1602 records the burial of John, the son of William Tylsley, a 'nayler'. Between this date and 1687 the names of a further twenty-eight nailers appear and it is likely that the trade developed not much later than in Dudley. Bromsgrove was an important centre of Worcestershire life and the fact that John Leland makes no reference to nailmaking ('Bromsgrove standeth somethinge by clothinge') does not necessarily mean the trade was not known in the area in the mid-sixteenth century. Leland made no mention of Birmingham's cloth and tanning trades either but it is known they employed a lot of people!

The Quarter Sessions Rolls also contain references to nailers in neighbouring areas such as Alvechurch, Chaddesley, Hagley, Pedmore, Northfield and Elmley Lovett. Belbroughton, renowned for its scythemakers, we know had nailers too, not from these rolls but from the parish registers where in 1596 there is a reference to Thomas Wheler whose father John was a nailer.

From the accounts of one of the guilds of Stratford, detailing the cost of various building repairs, it is possible to speculate about even earlier beginnings for the nail trade in the Bromsgrove area:

1397/8	1000	broddus	12d
1405	1000	nayles	18d
1469	4000	lath-nayles	10d per 1000 [12]

'Brads' and lath nails were later known to be specialities of Bromsgrove nailmakers. On the other hand John Cotton quotes the traditional story of St Ecguin of the ninth century who 'hearing an unfavourable account of the moral condition of Alcestrians' set out with other missionaries from Evesham to effect some reform. The saint and his companions were greeted with such a deafening clamour from the sound of hammers on anvils that they had to retreat unheard.[13] So perhaps the brads and lath nails came from Alcester, certainly a lot nearer to Stratford.

The seventeenth century was a period of growth with the more efficient exploiting of iron ore and coal. As the great iron ore centre of Sussex declined the West Midlands continued to rise. Charcoal, needed for smelting iron, was already scarce and easy access to local coal gave the region's nailers a head start. In fact the iron-making industry continued to use charcoal and only took wholeheartedly to coal in the second half of the eighteenth century—despite a certain Dud Dudley's claim to have made iron with coal in the 1620s.[14] But in the metal trades, including nailing, the use of coal continued to spread. The Black Country coal-workings were extended: some of the coal was still close to the surface and when this source was worked out coalmining went deeper, the problems of digging deep answered by Thomas Newcomen's engine in the early 1700s.[15] Either way, under foot or deep down, the nailers of the West Midlands were close to cheap supplies of coal and already the leading nail producers in the country.

The really great leap forward in the nailing industry came from the introduction of the slitting mill, the most important technical invention in the history of handmade nails. Up till its invention the preparation of the iron used by the nailers was time-consuming, involving the reduction, by hammering and cutting with shears, of a large block of iron to the required shapes and sizes. The slitting mill, introduced from Liège into Kent before the end of the sixteenth century, now did all this for the nailer.[16] Driven by water power the machine hammered—and by the end of the seventeenth century rolled—the iron into sheets and cut or slit them into rods or bars for sale to the nailer and smith.

Richard Foley is credited with the introduction of the Midlands' first slitting mill in 1628 at Stourbridge; but stories of his fiddling (or fluting) his way through Sweden (or Holland) posing as a spy (or idiot) in order to bring back the industrial secrets of the Europeans must be discounted as the evidence of the slitting mill's earlier introduction into Kent is much weightier.[17] Perhaps, as has been suggested, these stories stem from a desire on the part of Foley's descendants to find some sort of romantic origins since the Foley family was raised to the peerage in the early eighteenth century.

Slitting mills increased and the Stour, which joins the Severn south of Bewdley, became particularly important to the iron slitters. By the end of the eighteenth century this little river (no more than a stream really) had a higher concentration of slitting mills, forges and furnaces than any other English river of a similar length.[18]

The fame of the West Midlands nailers increased too and a very

Slitting rod iron (from Encyclopédie des Sciences, des Arts et des Métiers, 1773)

important export trade began to build up. The advent of the slitting mill led to cheaper and more abundant nails which in turn stimulated further demand. It also meant that the earlier manual skills required to hammer and cut a large block of iron—a *bloom* weighing between 30 and 40 lbs— into sizes and shapes suitable for nailmaking were no longer needed; the slitting mill produced rods of the necessary cross-section and all the nailer had to do was reduce these to shorter lengths and shape them into nails.

Not suprizingly the number of nailers increased. The trade had long earned the reputation for being easy to get into. It is interesting, for example, that there is no reference at all to a nailer's apprenticeship in the Quarter Sessions Rolls. This is not to say that there were no apprentices—instances like the three below prove otherwise:[19]

16th March 1668	*'William Stokes Son of Garvis Stokes was bound to John Wilson, Nailer, for 7 years from the 2nd of Feb(ruar)y. Parish gave 40s(hillings).'*
11th June 1670	*'Thomas Hemus was bound Apprentice to Matthew Wilson of Belbroughton, Nailer, for 7 years from the date being the eighth instant. the Parish gave xxxxs(hillings) with the said apprentice the Mother xxs(hillings) & 2 suits of apparrell.'*
February 14th 1789	*'Charles Tilt to John Marson, Bromsgrove Nailer.'*

But nailmaking, it was felt, was easy to learn; it went on in scattered areas away from the restricting influences of the old guilds and once the slitting mill arrived very little was needed in the way of equipment—a small forge to heat the rod, tongs, hammers and a nailblock, all easy to house in an outhouse or workshop added to the cottage. 'It was almost fatally easy for anyone born in or near the Black Country to join the ranks of this badly organized, casually conducted nail-maker's trade.'[20] And why not? Demand was still rising in Britain and abroad, there was plenty of work to do and, despite its poor working conditions, probably a memory of nailers of not so very long before who had done well—like the famous Richard Foley's father. And to the poor farmer, even worse off according to Richard Baxter, minister at Kidderminster, than the poor craftsman, it must have been a welcome escape route from the worry of uncertain tenure.

But it was all *too* easy to make nails. Too many men before long were making too many nails, supplies outstripped demand, prices dropped and poorly paid nailers found themselves having to work longer hours to make ends meet. The decline into poverty continued through the eighteenth century.

Nails were still in great demand though and the nailers' constant need for iron and coal was instrumental in the development of both these great West Midlands industries during the seventeenth and eighteenth centuries. Technically, apart from the effects of the slitting mill, the nailer's craft changed hardly at all over the centuries; but comparatively primitive though it was it played a vital part in the revolution in iron and coal simply because it required so much of the raw materials. All iron articles were in demand—mule- and horseshoes, chains and anchors, agricultural implements and a hundred and one types of nail. Pressure on the nail trade came from government departments, industry and shipping and trade with the colonies; and America became the biggest overseas customer, needing an immense number of nails for houses built from wood yet experiencing a severe shortage of labour.

Nailing was a ubiquitous trade: in lots of different centres in the West Midlands, both large and small, all sorts of nails were being made. There was no division of labour but gradually specialisation took place, the different nailmaking areas concentrating on different nails so that by the nineteenth century it was possible to differentiate, for example, between the products of over twenty nailmaking districts in the Black Country. The following areas became the generally accepted specialists in the nails listed:

Bromsgrove	hobs, brush nails, tacks, brads, clinkers
Dudley	mule- and horseshoe nails, frost cogs
Halesowen	spikes, pipe nails
Rowley Regis	rivets, hobs, small nails
Sedgley	gate nails, rose nails, spikes

Bromsgrove was noted for its small work as early as 1813. The Flemish tack, which the district turned out in its billions, was so small that a thousand weighed only 5 oz. When Princess Victoria visited the area in 1832 she was presented with a thousand such tacks in a goose's quill.[21] One wonders what she did with them.

According to some estimates provided for Matthew Boulton in 1785 by people in the trade, out of approximately 12,000 tons of iron being rolled and slit each year in the West Midlands nailmaking consumed between three-quarters and four-fifths;[22] and possibly as many as one-third of the workers (about 25-30,000) were women and children under fourteen years of age,[23] a situation unimaginable in the sixteenth century and rare in the seventeenth. By now whole families were working in the nailer's forge and, though demand for nails was particularly brisk as a result of the Napoleonic Wars, wages were not keeping up with inflation and longer hours were being worked for the same rewards.

Deteriorating relations with America, culminating in war and the break of 1812, dealt a great blow to the West Midlands nailers. Unsold stocks piled up and nailers were laid off. Many of those who kept working did so on reduced wages. All the worst features of the trade—poor conditions, long hours, low wages and the absence of any communal action to improve things (present for at least two hundred years)—grew more marked as the nineteenth century progressed. The leading craft in the iron industry was in its death throes. Significantly, the nailmakers of Birmingham had already moved on to better paid and more attractive trades, involving more highly finished products requiring greater skill. Prominent in the sixteenth century (when John Leland visited), Birmingham nailers, according to Hutton, had almost disappeared by the mid-eighteenth century.[24] And in the nineteenth century the same thing was happening in the Black Country, the number of nailers declining as they moved to better paid work. Even in Dudley—more fortunate than most since that area specialized in horseshoe nails, its nailers regarded as kings of the trade, highly skilled and among the last to be threatened by the machine-cut nail—the number of nailers had by 1840 greatly decreased. There was better money to be made in the nearby ironworks and mines.

But the people of Bromsgrove stuck to nails, continuing for many years to scratch a living out of them. They had no real choice: there were few alternative openings. Mr Benjamin Sanders' new button factory was employing over 300 (largely female) by the 1830s and the following decade saw the opening of the Wagon Works in Aston Fields. But the numbers employed added up to not much more than one-tenth of the number of nailers in the area at the industry's mid-century peak. Not until the first decade of the twentieth century was there a real alternative to nails when Herbert Austin began to make cars within striking distance of the town. For a large part of the nineteenth century, though—and for men in particular—it was nailing or nothing.

The first figures we have for numbers employed in the Bromsgrove nailing trade come from John Lacey in 1778 who noted that 'as near as can be computed' there were

> *In the Linnen about 180*
> *In the Nailing   900*
> *In the Linsey   140* [25]

There is a lot of guesswork about all population and occupational figures before the nineteenth century but if Lacey is anywhere near right Bromsgrove was chock-a-block with nailers, nearly a thousand out of a probable population of nearly 4650 (also Lacey's estimate, possibly conservative). Well-established by the seventeenth century—perhaps earlier—nailing had become Bromsgrove's staple trade well before the end of the eighteenth century. 'The Nailing business', wrote Lacey, 'chiefly implys (employs) the greatest part of the poor and is very brisk.'

At the very beginning of the nineteenth century the centre of the industry was probably still in the Black Country; in the years that followed the centre very definitely shifted to Bromsgrove, the last great nailing district of all. There is a unique and revealing entry in Bentley's History and Directory of Bromsgrove of 1840. Bromsgrove's inhabitants are listed under their private addresses and again under their trades or professions. The nailmakers get their heading all right, but then this paragraph underneath:

> (See Alphabetical Directory, the number is 538 and forms
> nearly one-half of the entire list, so it is unnecessary to give
> the names again here.)

The number 538 represents the heads of households, not total workers employed. That was far higher, 3042, nearly six times as many.[26] According to Alfred Palmer, founder of The Bromsgrove and Droitwich Weekly Messenger, each nailer in 1860 was making on average 2500 nails a day which means the nailing population must have been producing some 6,250,000 nails a day, over 30,000,000 a week.[27] In his introduction to his brand new directory he quotes a recent conversation with a local nailer:

> I have this day made 3000 nails and struck 64000 blows with
> my hammer.[28]

Until the bates (wage reductions) of the late 1830s the nailers were not outwardly disgruntled. They were resigned to a 70/80 hour week and were still their own masters in the sense that they could decide how long a day to work. They managed, somehow, to survive on the few shillings a week they earned. A few even reached a position of some comfort, judging from the will of Thomas Liddell of Bournheath (see Appendix E). But their independence was illusory and after the mid-century even the number of nailers in the Bromsgrove area was in decline. The introduction of machinery was eating more and more into the traditional home market of the wrought nail trade. London dock companies had long been good customers, for example, the East India Dock Company alone contracting annually for 110 tons of handmade nails; but by the mid-1860s most of the nails being bought by the company were made by machine. In the same way the Admiralty, for years purchasers of over 600 tons of handmade nails per annum, required only a very small quantity by the mid-60s. At the same time technological developments abroad meant the loss of demand in America, the colonies and parts of Europe. Belgium, difficult though it is to understand, managed to produce small nails, especially tacks, even more cheaply out of working and social conditions every bit as dire. And in the 1880s, to make matters even worse, Germany began exporting wire nails into Britain at a cheaper price than British handmade nails.

By 1900 there were less than a thousand nailers left in Bromsgrove. Joseph Gwynne, for some time neighbouring Alvechurch's solitary nailer, died in 1896 at the age of 76. Only 40 years earlier there had been ten workshops in full work, employing some 50/60 men.[29] The First World War drew more men away and on the eve of the Second World War there were few people left in the trade. Only a handful of men were making handmade nails in Bromsgrove by the time that war had finished. The story of the industry's demise is not a very happy one.

Two   Masters, foggers and truck

*The industry of nailmaking is profitable only to those who do not make them;
to this the luxurious houses and carriages of the nail-masters eloquently testify.
And to become a nailmaster requires neither knowledge, nor brains, nor capital.
Anybody with a few pounds to start with can enter this business.*

So wrote Robert Sherard after his visit to Bromsgrove in 1896.[1] To
succeed, he went on, 'apparently nothing is needed except an entire absence
of the altruistic sense'. All that had to be done was to rent a small warehouse,
buy a weighing machine, employ a man at 14/- to look after everything,
write a few business letters, take an occasional trip to nearby markets—and
leave the nailers to do the rest.

It's a little sweeping as a summary. For one thing a man—or woman—
needed a few brains to see the opportunity and set up as a nailmaster; more
to the point he *did* need a little capital, certainly an amount of money which
a nailmaker would readily describe as capital, the 'few pounds' which he
could never hope to accumulate. It is clear too that not all nailmasters were
parasites as Sherard would have people believe. The small group of larger
masters who met regularly to determine the price of nails had a reputation
for fair dealing and usually tried to discourage other 'smaller' masters and
foggers from paying below the list price and from operating the truck system.
In 1842, for example, at a quarterly meeting at Dudley, they entreated those
undercutting to pay the full amount, which they argued was already low
enough, and prevent further distress; and they pledged themselves to try
to put down the truck system, promising to employ all those nailers who
informed against foggers and masters paying in truck. There is plenty of
evidence to show that a number of local nailmasters were well thought of
by those who worked iron for them.

On the other hand, it could be argued they were weak since so often, after initial resistance, they cut back their own prices on the grounds that it was the only way they could compete with the numerous smaller men. The respectable masters, like the nailers, ultimately failed to organize themselves into a body strong enough to resist the spoilers of the trade, the undercutting middlemen. The story of nailing in the nineteenth century is the story of a complex triangle of relationships, a social and economic conundrum that was never solved.

The relationship between the nailmaker and his employer was an unusual one (most easily understood perhaps by today's paid home knitter than the rest of us). The nailmaster (or nail manufacturer or nail ironmonger as he was often known) stood between the nailer and the market. He bought iron rod from an ironmaster, handed it out in bundles to the nailers, paid for every bundle of hand-wrought nails returned and then proceeded to sell the products to the domestic consumer and export merchant. The iron was supplied in bundles of nail rod weighing 60 lbs and the nailmaster would tell the nailer exactly what type and size of nail was required. Once the nails were finished the nailer would return them to the nailmaster's warehouse—usually within eight days—and be paid accordingly. There was an allowance for wastage, particularly high for the finer and smaller nails (which Bromsgrove specialized in), from between 5 and 15/16 lbs per bundle.

Generally, when there was plenty of work, the nailer would deal with a single master; at other times he was forced to go from one master to another in search of work, the notice 'No Iron' dreaded but usually accepted without argument. Though cheating on both sides was rife a reasonably amicable relationship could exist between the good master and the good nailer, the former paying the agreed price, neither resorting to truck nor cheating with false weights, (and good for a 'sub' from the following week's wages); the nailer himself on time with his work and resisting the temptation to embezzle his employer's materials. To make sure they were not getting less than they should the nailmakers could enlist the aid of a crude set of balances and, failing this, a *bibble* , a stone of a certain weight.*

The temptation for the nailer to buy his iron outright from a nailmaster and sell to another or on the open market, in the hope of making a bit more money, was always present. But the nailmaster was not enamoured

* Among my prized possessions are the *bibble* and stone anvil given me by Wesley Perrins, Black Country historian and former MP.

with this bit of initiative which in any case, strictly speaking, was illegal. As far back as 1702 a statute of Queen Anne was enacted in an attempt to prevent fraud by workers in the cloth and iron trades and anyone found guilty faced a stiff penalty. If the nails were not returned within the prescribed time the nailer could be (and often was) hauled before a magistrate to be charged with neglect of service or breach of contract.

> Friday, by Tho(ma)s Holbeche Esq., and the Rev. Mr Pyndar, William Lee—to hard labour for one month for neglecting to work a quantity of rod iron into nails, the property of Tho(ma)s Binns of Bromsgrove.[2]

On the same day that William Lee was being dealt with the magistrates sentenced John Yarnold to hard labour for one month for similarly failing to return his nails in time, the property of Thomas Juggins of Bromsgrove.[3] So the frauds went on, the practice amongst nailers of selling direct to the market becoming so prevalent by the end of the eighteenth century that the nailmasters met to decide how to stop it. Their method was to 'remind' nailmakers of the precise letter of the law and publish these reminders in all the warehouses.

There is evidence that the nailers still continued to get iron from one master and sell their nails elsewhere. But the penalties were severe and on the whole the masters' action seems to have been moderately effective. Even so, the following report from the *Worcestershire Guardian* (22 December 1838) shows that at that late stage the Bromsgrove nailer was not averse to a bit of 'law bending':

> **Bromsgrove Petty Sessions**
> Thomas Jones and William Edwards, nailors, were convicted by having iron from their employer Mr H Ellins, and worked it out for other masters contrary to the statute in that case made and provided.
> Mr Ellins having forgiven them for the same offence once before, they were committed to the house of correction and to hard labour: Jones for two calendar months, and Edwards for six weeks.

Had the relationship between nailmaster and nailmaker continued to be a direct one there would have been considerably less friction. But in some districts this kind of relationship came to be less the norm as the nine-

THE NAIL IRONMONGERS,

At their GENERAL MEETING, held JANUARY 14th, 1800,—

FINDING IT NECESSARY TO CORRECT MANY GREAT ABUSES PRACTICED
IN THE TRADE,

UNANIMOUSLY RESOLVED TO PUBLISH THE FOLLOWING

ABSTRACTS,

From Acts of Parliament, for the proper Regulation of the Nail Trade.

ALL Nailors that receive Stock, or Stocks of Iron from their Master or Masters, are the Servants of the Person or Masters who delivered them the said Stock or Stocks, to work up into Nails, &c.

All Stocks of Iron not properly worked up and returned within eight Days, are declared by Law embezzled Stocks.

All Stocks of Iron, whether worked up or not, if sold, exchanged, or pawned, are also declared by the Law embezzled Stocks.

All Nailors that do not properly work up and return the Stock or Stocks of Iron delivered to them by their Master, Masters, or Agents, within eight Days after receiving the same, or that exchange it, or work it up for any other Person, or sell it, or pawn it, or dispose of it in any Manner whatever, to any other Person than to the Master or Masters, he, she, or they received it from, shall forfeit double the Value of such Stock, with all Expences, or be committed to Bridewell to hard Labour for three Months, and publicly whipped, (for the Embezzlement only.)

Every Nailor that receives a Stock of Iron from any Master or Masters, and before the Expiration of eight Days, or before he has worked up and completed the said Stock, doth, or shall apply for and receive a Stock of Iron from any other Person or Persons, shall be committed to Bridewell for three Months.

Every Nailor that receives a Stock of Iron from any one Master to work up, cannot suffer himself to be retained or employed by any Occupation or Business whatever, before he has worked up and completed the same, without being liable to three Months' Imprisonment.

Any Nailor receiving Iron to work up into Nails, that shall wilfully damnify, spoil, destroy, or improperly manufacture the said Iron, shall forfeit double the Value thereof, or be committed to Prison for three Months.

Every Factor, Carpenter, Shoe-maker, Shop-keeper, Blacksmith, or any other Person whatever, that takes or receives Iron or Nails, wrought or unwrought, either by Gift, Pledge, Sale, or Exchange, from any Person or Persons known to be employed in working up the same, (the Consent of the Employer not being first had) shall, on Conviction thereof, forfeit *Forty Pounds*, not less than *Twenty*, or suffer three Months' Imprisonment.

Any Person who shall sell, pawn, or exchange, or otherwise dispose of Materials for Manufacture, whether wrought or unwrought, not being properly authorised to dispose of the same, shall suffer the like Punishment as for receiving them.

All Wages to Workmen are required to be paid in good and lawful Money, and not with Goods, or in any other way, under a Penalty of *Ten Pounds*, Half of which Fine to be paid to the Informer, the other Half to the Person so paid.

Any Nailor threatening his Employer, or any of his Property, is guilty of Felony.

Any Materials delivered to be manufactured, whether wrought or unwrought, suspected to be embezzled, (if concealed) may be searched for in the Day Time, in any House, or Premises whatever.

teenth century wore on. Keeping a warehouse meant a lot of paperwork for the nailmaster, giving out iron and collecting the wrought nails required eagle-eyed supervision to prevent the nailers from stealing, and the wide range of nails in demand meant large stocks had to be kept which could lead to great losses in times of economic difficulties. At the same time badly paid nailers were usually in need of money, often so much in debt they would take work on more or less any terms. Between them they allowed a kind of nail factor, a middleman, to emerge centre stage who came to stand for everything bad in the trade—long hours, low wages and truck—the *fogger*.

The fogger employed nailers and sold the handmade nails to the nailmasters. From the latter's point of view the fogger had his uses. He could provide the nailmaster with particular kinds of nails when needed—and at short notice—thus relieving the need to carry large stocks; and his activities meant a reduction in bookkeeping and in the need to supervise nailers. The fogger thus took on some of the nailmaster's risk as well as the time-consuming duties involved in dealing directly with the nailers.

It has to be said that the fogger, reviled as he was, also proved useful to the nailer, often giving him work when he had spent his wages too quickly and couldn't exist until the nailmaster next opened his warehouse (once, at the most twice, a week), or when the nailmaster's 'No Iron' sign was up. The less honest nailer also shored up the fogger's position by going to him when no nailmaster would employ him. From the fogger he could get a little bit of iron and return a few nails at any time. The fogger thrived therefore because both masters and men made use of him and because he was able without difficulty to find room to operate in a trade which, though in decay, was still very overcrowded and from the 1830s beginning to feel the competition of the machine-made nail.

Not that the fogger was unique to the nineteenth century. He came into his own then but he was around much earlier than that. As far back as 1621 a Bill was drafted 'for the reformation of sundry abuses committed by diverse evil disposed persons that engross and get into their own hands great store of victuals and other commodities, and exchange the same at unreasonable rates with poor handicraftsmen that work in iron and steel within the several counties of Stafford, Salop, Wigorn (Worcestershire), and Warwick'. Significantly, the Bill is endorsed: 'Bill concerning the nailers'. Was there ever a golden age in the trade? Perhaps in the sixteenth century—certainly by the seventeenth the awful truck system was already well established.

The nineteenth-century fogger did not carry as much or as varied a stock as the nailmaster; and in many instances he did not pay in cash for the nails but by a ticket or token (not, incidentally, to be confused with the token coin of the seventeenth, eighteenth and early nineteenth centuries which among manufacturers was both legal and much more widely acceptable). As earlier legislation made clear, wages were supposed to be paid 'in good and lawful Money, and not with Goods, or in any other way'.[4] But the practice of paying with tokens exchangeable only for the fogger's own over-priced goods continued and just what it meant in terms of lower wages and dearer goods was very ably set out in two letters to the Bromsgrove and Droitwich Weekly Messenger in the spring of 1862:

THE TRUCK SYSTEM
To the Editor of the Bromsgrove and Droitwich Weekly Messenger.

SIR,—You will much oblige by publishing the accompanying statements, which I am prepared to prove to be correct.

I am, Sir,
Yours truly,
WM. LAUGHER

Bromsgrove
April 4th, 1862.

A Master's Price.

2 lb. hobs 7¼d. per thousand.
20 oz. best Flemish, 8½d.
20 oz. fine Battin, 7d.
2 lb. best Clout, 9½d.

A Truck Shop.

	s	d
4 lbs. bacon, 10d. per lb	3	4
3 lbs. cheese, 9d. per lb	2	3
2 lbs. butter, 14d. per lb	2	4
1 lb. soap, 6d. per lb	0	6
2 lbs. lard, 10d. per lb	1	8
2 lbs. sugar, 6d. per lb	1	0
	11	1

A Fogger's Price.

2 lb. hobs, 6d. per thousand
20 oz. best Flemish, 6d.
20 oz. fine Battin, 6d.
2 lb. best Clout, 7d.

A Grocer's Shop.

	s	d
4 lbs. bacon, 6d. per lb	2	0
3 lbs. cheese, 6d. per lb	1	6
2 lbs. butter, 1s. per lb	2	0
1 lb. soap, 3d. per lb	0	3
2 lbs. lard, 7d. per lb	1	2
2 lbs. sugar, 5d. per lb	0	10
	7	9

THE TRUCK SYSTEM—*To the Editor of the Bromsgrove and Droitwich Weekly Messenger*—

SIR—In your paper of April 5th, there appeared a statement showing a master's price and a fogger's price, the cost of goods at a truck shop and a grocer's shop. Now sir, I am about to show, and am prepared to prove (if required) the plans used by the truck-seller. As soon as the workman enters the warehouse, there stands the truck-seller ready to put on the "screw": he commences to count the nails, and soon finds fault—they are too large or too small, &c. There stands the workman, who dares not to lift his head. The truck-seller says, "I cannot give you the price for them, if I buy them I must have them at twopence off," meaning twopence per thousand under the masters' price. The man is dumb, knowing that the fogger has him in his power, and is obliged to submit. After weighing the nails, still putting on the "screw", a little performance in the truck-shop follows. "Now," says the truck-seller, "hold out your hand"; then, placing the money in the hand of the workman, says at the same time, "Give it me again," and so it quickly returns to its former owner. This they call paying a man his money. Between the low price of the nails and the high price of the truck, I am confident the workmen cannot receive more than twelve shillings in the pound! Under these acts of injustice the operative cannot live and pay his way: families are starving, landlords are crying aloud for rent and the tenant has none to give. Contrast the truck nail buyer with the operative nail maker:—the one is up to his eyes in bricks and mortar, the other after sixty years' labour has not saved himself enough to buy a shroud. Sir, as we have the sympathy of the clergy and gentry of the town and of our respectable shopkeepers and tradesmen, who have promised to help us in our just struggle, I hope the day is not far distant when the word truck will cease to be heard.—I remain, sir, your obedient servant, WM. LAUGHER, April 17th, 1862.

The 'little performance' William Laugher refers to presumably represented the deeply cynical observation of the letter of the law while the spirit was being severely clouted. Some foggers had not only truck (or tommy) shops and pubs but bakers and boot and shoe shops so that not a penny of the nailers escaped their clutches. One witness before the Truck Commission complained that the truckmaster's flour 'was not fit for a pig to eat . . . and 8d dearer'.[5]

The fogger was the greatest blight on Bromsgrove's landscape; no trick was too despicable for him. He stooped, in some instances, to boring a hole in the base of the weight and filling it with lead so that the nailer had

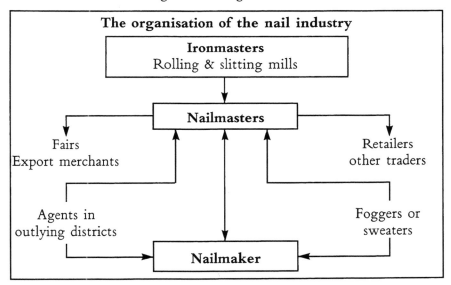

to provide over the odds. On other occasions he would resort to deliberately providing the nailer with bad iron so that the price paid for the finished nails would be cut and the nailer receive less for his pains than anticipated. At times he would also supply the wrong-sized iron for the particular nails which forced the nailer to go to an iron changer, paying 1d or 2d for every bundle corrected—and the iron changer was not always unrelated to the fogger! Sometimes he refused to allow nailers to carry their own completed nails to the warehouse, instead charging him high carriage costs.

A letter to the Bromsgrove and Droitwich Weekly Messenger on 17 August 1863 points out that a nail fogger from Shaver's End in Dudley had just been charged with possessing unjust weights. The heavier weights had been found to be too heavy, the lighter weights too light. The heavier weights were used for nails paid by weight, the lighter for nails paid by weight per thousand. Thus, however he was paid the nailer would lose out, the fogger cheating on both counts. The letter was signed 'A Victim'.

All these were blatant violations of existing legislation. The assertion that the Truck Act of 1831—the result of culminating anti-truck riots of earlier that year—probably averted revolution, so great were the evils of the system, can hardly be supported since the Act completely evaded the issue of enforcement and truck continued for many years after. It was too easy to get round the Act: the fogger's threat that there would be no more work if the nailer's wages were not spent in his shop seems to have been very effective—as the Select Committee on Sweating discovered in 1888 when it was told by no less a person than the Secretary of the Nailmakers Association that the inspectors were 'not up to this dodge' (*ie* clever doctoring of the balances) and that fear of losing his job would stop him from telling an inspector. Not until the second Truck Act were inspectors appointed to enforce legislation; and even for a while after that the system went on.

But for most of the nineteenth century the nailer was getting the worst of both worlds from the fogger: as a worker having to accept below the rate, as a consumer having to buy at above. During the strike of 1863 a lengthy article appeared in the Birmingham Daily Post of 25 June. Its author clearly regarded the truck system as the biggest evil in the nailing trade, a system which had given birth to 'a kind of bastard trader . . . called by himself a "factor"; by his neighbours, not being nailers, a "tommy-master", or a "truck-master"; and by the nail makers, who suffer by him, a "fogger"—the diminutive, probably, of "pettifogger". The article went on:

> He gave out his iron to the nail maker, who manufactured it and brought it home. He then paid for the work not wholly in cash, but for the most part by a ticket for provisions, which ticket could only be honoured at his own shop. By this ingenious *ruse* he succeeded in getting a double advantage. In the first place, he paid the nail maker with goods bought on credit, and could therefore afford to give credit to the "market master"; and in the second place he charged the nail maker an exorbitant price for his provisions, and pocketed large profits. Where he was the proprietor of a public house as well as a shop he throve still better. In that case he could keep the men

waiting for their iron at the beginning of the week, and for
their tickets at the end of it, and, as waiting in that district
means drinking, he reaped large profits . . .

Thus the truck system was the perfect monopoly. While making the
fogger very comfortable it forced the nailer to buy in a non-competitive
market; it meant his wages could be lowered at any stage simply by
increasing the price of truck goods (or lowering their quality); it kept him
in poverty, took away his pride and self-respect because he rarely ate well,
dressed properly or lived comfortably; and it denied him the chance to
save, to build a better future.

Lord Brougham said we ought to put something by in our
young days so that we need not go to the parish when we
were old. Well, are we to put by the rotten goods? If this
did not come from a lord, one would say his brains were
as rotten as the goods that our work is paid in.

The above extract is from a letter written by a handweaver near
Huddersfield and published in the Northern Star on 27 April 1843, but
it could equally have come from a Bromsgrove nailer.

General anti-truck societies were formed in Bromsgrove in the 1830s.
The chairman of one of them, Rev Dr Collis, headmaster of Bromsgrove
School, offered a reward of £5 to anyone giving him evidence he could use
to bring an action against the offender. There was evidence in abundance
but the offer was not immediately taken up: it would almost certainly have
meant loss of work for the informing nailer. Not until 1863 was the
Nailmakers Anti-Truck Society set up with Job Davies as its chairman. At
the Society's inaugural meeting (reported in the Bromsgrove and
Droitwich Weekly Messenger on 12 September 1863) the general public
was left in no doubt about the reason for its formation.

. . . for the sole purpose of employing every lawful means
of annihilating that nefarius system of Truck by which the
nailors and their families have been so long and deeply
injured; and which threatens the utter extinction of all
legitimate trade.

The final clause shows a foresight which had not penetrated the conciousness of the nailmasters—and would not do so until the 1891/2 strike.

Truck survived so long because in an overcrowded trade nailers were never in any position of strength to complain and the efforts of anti-truck societies and reputable masters were unavailing. In the opinion of the local inspector for Bromsgrove, quoted in the Truck Commission Report of 1871, the nailers who worked under the fogger 'were a low dejected lot compared with the others'.

The nailmasters meanwhile were growing increasingly anxious about a different threat to the hand-wrought nail trade, the nail machine. A great many patents for nailmaking machines were taken out in the late eighteenth and early nineteenth century, particularly in America (over twenty by 1800) where labour was dear and the need for nails great. Nail machines of one sort or another were in operation there before 1830; but though a number of patents were granted in this country, including several in the Birmingham area (among the earliest some for making several nails that Bromsgrove specialized in, such as tacks and hobs), there was less interest in Britain because labour was so cheap.

In 1830 however new machinery was introduced and nail factories were established for the first time. Though only a few types of nails could be made by machine in the early years nevertheless the effect on the hand-made nail industry was considerable. Competition became even stiffer in the 1860s when further technological improvements were made in cut-nail manufacturing, enabling more types, like the horseshoe nail for example, to be made by machine. Machine-cut nails cornered even more of the home market in the 1880s when cheap basic steel began to be used.

Much of the information concerning the nailmasters of the first half of the nineteenth century comes from the trade directories, very important sources for the decades when there was no local newspaper. From the earliest of these we find just six masters listed in Bromsgrove (all called nail ironmongers), a low number in view of the fact that production of hand-wrought nails must have been very considerable at this time; and there are no masters at all in Catshill or Bournheath.

It must be stressed, however, that directories tell only part of the story—and that not always accurately. For instance, there is evidence that more nailmasters and factors were in business than the different lists suggest (why some names were omitted we don't know); there were probably one or two more non-Bromsgrove nail manufacturers in the area than the directories lead us to believe; and there is an outstanding example in

Bromsgrove Nailmasters in 1820

George Gabb	Victualler & Wholesale Nail Ironmonger	Victoria High Street
Henry Hellens	Wholesale Nail Ironmonger & Linen Manufacturer	High Street
Thomas Juggins	Nail Ironmonger	High Street
Sanders & Blew	Nail Ironmongers	High Street
Scroxton & Broady	Nail Ironmongers	St John Street
Jabez Stanley	Nail Ironmonger	Strand

From: Lewis's Worcestershire Directory 1820

Billing's Directory and Gazeteer of the County of Worcester, 1855) where the provider of information to the editor just did not know the terminology, every nail 'person' listed as a 'factor'with one exception— Rock & Co, a Cradley firm of nail manufacturers whose title the directory got right presumably because the firm took out a half-page advertisement!

By 1835 the number of nailmasters had doubled and included two in Catshill, John Roberts and Jeffrey Ward.[6] From 1840[7] onwards a significant new catagory appears, the middlemen described as nail factors and including among their ranks the men universally known as foggers. From the two listed in Slater's Worcestershire Directory, 1850 (Samuel Taylor and David Troth, both of Sidemoor) the number rises dramatically to fifteen by 1865, nearly as many as there were nail manufacturers.

Masters and Middlemen in 1865

David Brazier	Wrought and Cut Nail Manufacturer	Station Street
William Cotton	Nail Factor	Sidemoor
William Crawford	Nail Manufacturer	Strand
Dipple & Kings	Ironmongers, Cutlers, Nail & Rivet Manufacturers, Cork Manufacturers, Ale & Porter Merchants	High Street
Joseph Dyer	Butcher & Nail Manufacturer	Sidemoor
James Green & Co	Wrought & Cut Nail Manufacturers	Strand
John Hanson	Innkeeper, Nail Factor, Boot & Shoe Maker	Rock Tavern
James Heague	Nail Factor	Worcester Street
Henry Ince	Beer Retailer & Nail Factor	Hundred House
George James	Nail Factor	Birmingham Road
Benjamin Johnson	Nail Manufacturer	High Street
Job Lewis	Shopkeeper & Nail Factor	Birmingham Road
Joseph Maskell	Nail Factor	Sidemoor

Masters and Middlemen in 1865 (cont.)

Amos Miles	Innkeeper, Nail Manufacturer, Iron Merchant, Coffin Loop Maker	King's Head
Henry Parry	Nail Manufacturer	Worcester Street
Thomas Penn	Nail Factor	High Street
James Penny	Nail Factor	The Putcheon, Stourbridge Road
Francis Perkins & Son	Nail Manufacturer	High Street
Edward Perkins	Nail Manufacturer	High Street
Richard Porter	Nail Factor	Sidemoor
William Powell	Nail Factor	Stourbridge Street
Samuel & John Price	Nail Manufacturer	Birmingham Road
Mrs Ann Ramsdale	Nail Factor & Shopkeeper	Birmingham Road
Scroxton & Brooke	Nail Manufacturer	St John Street
John Skidmore	Nail Manufacturer	Sidemoor
Samuel Taylor	Nail Manufacturer, Tea Dealer & Grocer	Sidemoor
Richard Troth	Nail Factor	Sidemoor
Samuel Troth	Nail Manufacturer	Sidemoor
Frederick William Turton	Nail Manufacturer & Insurance Agent	St John Street
Frederick Willis	Nail Factor	St John Street
Jabez Willis	Nail Factor & Shopkeeper	Hanover Street
John Witheford	Nail Manufacturer	High Street
Joseph Witheford	Nail Manufacturer	Hanover Street

From: Palmer's Bromsgrove Almanack and Directory, 1865

In addition to the above there were five nail factors in Bournheath (Benjamin Horton, George Moore, Peter Moore, Samuel Norbury and Abraham Webly)—approximately one to every twenty-five houses! And at Catshill there were two nail manufacturers (Enoch Hadley and Thomas Parry) and two factors (Benjamin Broomfield and Abraham Webley). The list demonstrates how highly competitive the trade had become and how large the factor/fogger loomed. It should almost certainly be longer: no mention is made, for example, of the firm of Eliza Tinsley which featured in the Bromsgrove nail trade for a number of years.

After the great nailers' strike of 1891/2 the trade went into a rapid decline. Alternative forms of employment were at last beginning to appear: the Austin Motor Company in 1905, for example, the Bromsgrove Guild and commercial market gardening. By the very last year of the nineteenth century there were fourteen nailmasters[8] and factors left in the area employing just under 1000 nailers. Just before the First World War the number had dwindled to ten; and by the time the world was drifting towards further hostilities there were just four nailmasters left.

The Nailmasters of 1937

Walter Kings	Nail Manufacturer & Nailmaker	Catshill
William Mason	Nail Manufacturer	High Street
James Parry	Nail Manufacturer	Catshill
Charles Troth	Nailmaker & Master	Sidemoor

From: Palmer's Bromsgrove Almanack and Directory, 1937

The old staple trade had almost gone. The people of Aston Fields had never got involved in the trade but instead had manned the Wagon Works and later the clothing factory. The people of Stoke Prior had long had the salt works. But many of the nailers in the town area had to stick to the

From Palmer's Bromsgrove Almanack and Directory 1860

trade until more opportunities presented themselves—the boracic lint mill at Charford in the 1870s, the large boot and shoe factory in the Worcester Road in the 1890s, the steam laundry in the Birmingham Road at the turn of the century; and as transport improved they were able to get to the industries of southern Birmingham, including the new car factory.

Nearly all the nailmasters listed as operating in the Bromsgrove area were local people. 'Up-country' masters, as outsiders were called, were on the whole the exception. One of these was a rather remarkable one, the Black Country firm of Eliza Tinsley & Co with Mrs Tinsley herself at its head for a number of years. It had warehouses in all parts of the Black Country and in Bromsgrove and Catshill as well; and the firm was still going strong for several decades in this century. Mrs Tinsley, a most respected nailmaster, was known as 'The Black Widow'. Just before her death in 1882 she employed over 4000 people.

Eliza Tinsley was not the earliest up-country firm to establish a footing in the Bromsgrove area. William Rock & Co of Cradley were already operating in Catshill in the 1850s. And the Halesowen firm of Homes and Hickton, 'manufacturers of best countersunk horse and every other description of wrought iron nails', also had a warehouse in Catshill.

John Roper of the High Street, a master with a good reputation, appeared in the 1870s. The firm was still operating in the 1930s as older Bromsgrovians will remember. One of Roper's warehouses still stands today at the back of Blunt's shoeshop in the High Street, down a court known as Crawford's or Brighton's Yard. The Catshill warehouse of the nailmaster James Parry, on the other hand, has recently been demolished. The Parry firm started as Thomas Parry before 1850 and may well be the longest-standing nail manufacturing establishment in the area since Parry was still in operation until 1940, one of the very last nailmasters in the area.

One of the most stable of all Bromsgrove's past nailmasters was James Green who began life as coffin, furniture makers and factors in the High Street in the early part of the last century, a few years later combining general factoring with nail manufacturing and then, towards the middle of the century, moved to the Strand. Some time after 1871 the baton was handed on and the firm renamed George Green & Co. The 'Green' presence in Bromsgrove was a long one—getting on for one hundred years. Perhaps such long-term survival had something to do with keeping up with industrial development: it was the first and for many years the only establishment to be described as a manufacturer of wrought and *cut* nails.

The firm's Strand warehouse stood next door to the old DD and SS Club.

From time to time other Greens featured in the nailing history of the area, the best known John Henry Green who managed the warehouse in Church Street for Eliza Tinsley and became chairman of the Nailmasters Association. The Association met (in its early years in Dudley, later in the Midland Hotel, Birmingham) to discuss the problems of the trade and to decide in particular on the prices to be paid to the nailer for his finished products and on prices charged to domestic and foreign buyers.

Another old Bromsgrove firm of nailmasters was Thomas Scroxton which first appeared in Lewis's Worcestershire Directory of 1820 in partnership with Broady, then as Thomas Scroxton in Pigot's 1835 trade directory, then as Scroxton and Brooke in Slater's Worcestershire Directory of 1850.* Nineteenth-century Bromsgrove fairly buzzed with Scroxtons. John Scroxton was the pastor of the Baptist Church for over thirty years, founder of probably the first Sunday School in the area. He lived in St John Street, at the age of eighty-four acting as a sub-distributor of stamps until his death four years later in 1854. His son, John Harris Scroxton, was a stationer and bookseller in the High Street, one of the town's earliest photographers and actively involved in the Mechanics' Institute. And then there was Miss Jane Scroxton who kept an infants' school in St John Street. Throughout the years the nail-manufacturing branch of the family operated in that same street on the site of what is now the market car park.

William Mason was the last central Bromsgrove nailmaster. He had warehouses in the High Street and in Worcester Road, the latter at the old British Legion headquarters (where 'Images' now is). There was also a warehouse in Catshill. The Mason firm existed from the early years of this century through to the late 1930s, operating in the last few years from the old button factory. The last legible entry in the firm's final accounts reads:

> *April 2nd 1937*
> *606   John Troth   19/7*

Of more personal siginificance is another slightly earlier payment:

> *December 19th 1936*
> *849   Kings   77 lbs clinkers   £2/1/8½* **

---

* I have a wonderful leather-bound traveller's case produced by Scroxton and Brooke given to me by Tim Brotherton who came across it in Wales. It now contains a sample of almost every kind of nail made in Bromsgrove.

**I've waited thirty years to broadcast this! It refers to my grandad, Jack Kings, the acknowledged expert on alpine clinkers and pig rings.

The return for making 77 lbs of clinkers was probably the result of 70 hours or more work. For 50 hours work a top toolmaker at Austin's was earning £3/2/0. In that same week in 1936 'Snaggy' Porter earned only £1/3/11. (Perhaps he put in a lot less hours!) The few nailers left on the Mason books were taken over in 1937 by John Nicholls who owned the button factory. They continued until 1945 to live precariously from a trade which to all intents and purposes was dead.

Another nailmaster, Walter Kings of Golden Cross Lane, was at work in Catshill until just after the last war, a nailmaker as well as master, and a keen lay preacher. But the honour of being the area's last surviving nailmaster must go to Charlie Troth of York Road in Sidemoor, a nailmaker who became his own nailmaster in 1937. He concentrated on making handmade brush nails and then swapped hats and sold them. He led a full, active life, another lay preacher in the trade, and carried on working until he was 76. He died ten years later in 1963.

Nailmasters and more particularly foggers often had other occupational strings to their bows. Over the years nail factors pursued a variety of additional jobs—like William Crawford in the 1870s who was described as a nail factor and cow-keeper.[9] The most popular combination was nail factoring and shop- or pubkeeping (the perfect way of course for the fogger to make sure he 'benefitted' from the nailer's earnings). In the 1850s, for example, James Harris hosted the Royal Oak at Wildmoor (or Little Catshill as it was called);[10] in the 1860s John Hanson, nail factor and boot and shoemaker, for good measure kept the Rock Tavern on Rock Hill; Henry Ince, nail factor, kept the Hundred House; and several other factors, like Samuel Taylor of Sidemoor, were shopkeepers (usually grocers).[11] In the 1870s George James of Norton on the Birmingham Road dealt in nails, kept a shop and ran a farm.[12]

Further up the social scale some of the nailmasters were not confining themselves to nails either. In the 1860s Amos Miles, nail manufacturer and coffin loop maker, had the King's Head in the High Street, a little down from the present Queen's Head. (In the previous decade he'd been mine host at the Bird in Hand, below today's Red Lion);[13] while Frederick Turton was a nail manufacturer, prosperous leather merchant (with a leather and grindery warehouse) and shopkeeper (boots and shoes, naturally).[14]

But there was a more unusual secondary activity which seems to have become quite a little tradition among nailmasters. Joseph Witheford of Hanover Street was 'Registrar of Marriages' in the 1850s and 1860s, a job taken on in the 1880s by James Laughton of the High Street and in the earlier years of this century by J A Brighton. Another nail manufacturer, Benjamin Johnson, was registering births and deaths in the town in the 1860s.

While the nineteenth-century makers of nails had little hope of escaping abject poverty, the sellers of their products appear to have been a prosperous group, some achieving a distinct measure of comfort, a position of some weight in the town. George Ellins, nail manufacturer in the High Street, had Rigby Hall built in 1838, about a mile away from the noise and dirt of the trade. The estate comprised 'a Mansion House, calculated for the residence of a gentleman's family, beautifully situate on an eminence, commanding rich and varied prospects of the adjacent country' (and so on and so forth)* —and was set in nearly twenty-five acres of land. Two years later, unfortunately for Mr Ellins, the railway came along and split the estate in two. He sold it in 1843.

Edward Perkins had his principal warehouse in the High Street for over 35 years. For some time he lived over his ironmonger's shop opposite the Golden Cross but moved, probably in the 1860s, to the Oakalls, a pleasant house 'with a capital garden and orchard'.[15] In the late 1850s Thomas

Rydal Mount, formerly Alma House, home of nailmaster Thomas Scroxton

* Estate agents' blurbs don't change much. This comes from Messrs Oates and Perrens who auctioned the estate.

Scroxton built Alma House on the Kidderminster Road, a handsome house just round the corner from his business in St John Street. He named the house patriotically after the battle of the Alma in 1854, the first encounter between the Allies and the Russians in the Crimean War. Later, the name of the house was changed to Rydal Mount.

Meanwhile James Green was repairing daily from his labours in the town to the Mount (up the lane from the United Reformed Church), a 'capital house and grounds'.[16] And Enoch Hadley made a good enough living out of nails to be able to purchase in the 1870s the Barnsley Hall estate with its commodious farmhouse and to send his son to Bromsgrove School. The latter (inevitably?) entered the professions, becoming a solicitor. Hadley's previous house, incidentally, was also substantial, the Brooklands on the Stourbridge Road.

Men like Enoch Hadley may have been part of an industry whose workers were generally held to be at the bottom of the trade heap; but the connection doesn't seem to have marred their social and civic standing. Hadley was a member of the Local Board (for the country district of Barnsley Hall), vice-chairman of the Board of Guardians of Bromsgrove Workhouse, a member of the Bromsgrove Savings Bank committee and treasurer of the Bromsgrove Temperance Society. Dan Roper was on the Town Distict Board in the 1880s; Joseph Witheford, when he wasn't registering marriages and manufacturing nails, was heavily involved in the work of the Mechanics' Institute. And James Parry, nail manufacturer of Worcester Street, reached the dizzy heights of inclusion in the mid-century list of 'Clergy and Gentry etc.'.[17]

In the second half of the nineteenth century a number of local nailmasters were members of the Board of Guardians—including Thomas Scroxton, Enoch Hadley, Joseph Witheford and Walter Parry—the body responsible for running the Union Workhouse built in 1838 (the building which was later to become the town's long-standing 'path lab'). Was altruism the nailmasters' motive for becoming involved in what at times—particularly during strikes—was a heavy rate-spending body? A cynic might argue it was probably more to do with a desire to ensure that the rates were spent as prudently as possible, that 'outdoor relief' (as payments out of the Poor Rate were called) was given sparingly to the Town's poorest citizens, many of them, of course, nailers. This generally niggardly attitude on the part of the Guardians was confirmed by Joby Leadbetter, a county councillor appointed to the Board towards the end of the last century when to be poor was still regarded as an offence.[18]

It would be more difficult, even for the naturally suspicious, to ascribe underhanded motives to the nailmasters'involvement in another aspect of the mid-nineteenth century life of the town, the Mechanics' Institute. The Institute was established in 1850, operating first from the corner of Stratford Road, later moving into the High Street. It aimed to advance the lot of the working classes by providing a library of books, journals and newspapers at a time when no other educational opportunities existed for the poor adults in the area; by offering classes in reading, writing and simple maths; and by laying on penny, and sometimes free, lectures on a variety of informative (and sometimes even entertaining!) topics. There were even some classes, presumably in response to demand, for children 'of tender years'.

Though not involved in its setting up, several nailmasters were involved in the Institute, particularly Edward Perkins and Joseph Witheford. Both were members of the Executive Committee, Perkins for some time its treasurer and over the years regularly in the chair, Witheford a long-serving secretary. When the Institute amalgamated with the Literary and Scientific Institution in 1862 Edward Perkins was its chairman and Joseph Witheford its secretary. And the minutes book [19]shows that at least some nailers took advantage of what it had to offer, several, like David Sandford, sitting on the Executive Committee working alongside their employers.

Throughout the 1850s the Institute must have been an educational oasis for the working man. But not for the working woman. Right from the start it was agreed she would be allowed in only on evenings when original papers were read. She was thus denied the chance of acquiring reading and writing skills and, more importantly perhaps, of passing them on to her children.

Three   One up, one down

Robert Sherard was clearly impressed with the Bromsgrove area when he visited it in the spring of 1896. Unlike the 'murky towns' of the Black Country, Bromsgrove was 'bright and sweet and clean, with many picturesque old houses and a fine old church, and all around it... some of the prettiest country in the Midlands'; the sort of place where a 'simple man, a God-fearing man... might be very happy'. On investigation, however, Sherard soon discovered that in the midst of this idyllic scene was embedded a real tragedy—the worst paid of all the 'white slaves' of England, the nailers.

> Off the principal street are numerous courts... one can pass
> in one minute from prosperous burgherdom to the lowest
> slavery.[1]

Running off the Strand, Rotten Row (as the bottom end of Stourbridge Road was known), the High Street, Worcester Street, Hanover Street and St John Street were over fifty entries, or *courts* as they were called. Each opening from the street led to an alley with a row or huddle of upward of half-a-dozen cottages, lavatories, bruhuses, *miskins* (brick-built rubbish dumps) and nailshops. Space permitting there might also be a crude pigeon loft.

These town courts were an essential part of Bromsgrove's industrial and social life throughout the nineteenth and early twentieth centuries, a number of them built on more ancient pathways that crisscrossed the main street. Some of the courts were *pudding bags* (cul-de-sacs), while others led through to back alleys or further courts. As time went on and children came to have more leisure they proved wonderful places for all sorts of games. And they acquired, inevitably, their own special names, more personal than the mere number by which each was officially designated. Often these names stemmed from the shop on the corner which accounts for some of the courts having two names. Opposite Lloyds Bank stood Depper's Alley (or Entry) which was also called Amiss's Yard. The next one down from there was Crawford's or Brighton's Yard named after the shoe shop on the corner. Round in Church Street were Malt House Square and Well Yard, all the courts mentioned so far leading down to Back Alley (or Lane), the road where the buses now stop. Further down the High Street, below the junction with New Road, Clegg's Entry retains its former name—from the owner of the

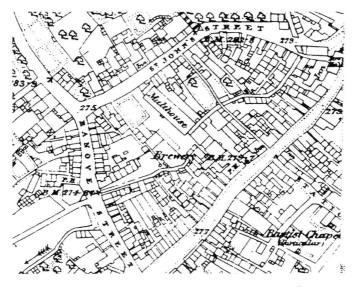

toy shop on the corner; but it was also known as Dipple's Entry. Some courts still remain, stripped of almost all their cottages under the 1937 Slum Clearance Act. A slightly higher percentage of the hostelries that served them have survived!

The site of the present market hall and car park once accommodated a maze of such courts as the map above—an enlargement of a section of the 1886 OS map—shows only too well. Note too the well-placed brewery and malthouse. For the children in the earlier decades of this century this was a fairy tale area for playing games such as bedlam, hopscotch, tip-cat, ay acky, strong-and-weak-horses and, on darker nights, white-horse-kick-back and button tapping. The more vigorous could venture across the road where the 48 steps up to the church presented challenges galore. A bike frame from the tip with a couple of pram wheels bolted onto the forks was a real treasure—and a way of coming down into St John Street at breakneck speed.

The only danger was the Co-op coal cart, Ted Hammond's milk float or 'Mish' Rowlands with his rag-and-bone trolley.

In the town centre the area bounded by the High Street, Mill Lane and Church Street contained within it over 70 nailers' cottages and several well known courts—Amiss's Yard, Brighton's Yard, Malt House Square and Well Yard. It had the reputation for being Bromsgrove's roughest part, more violent than 'Side Moor', 'Big Catshill' and Worcester Street (none of which were awfully choice either).

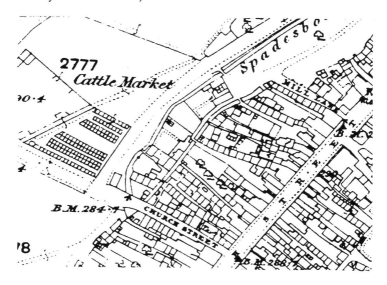

Another notable nailing area in the nineteenth and early twentieth centuries lay to the west of Stourbridge Street, now the Parkside car park with only the reconstructed Mitre building and the Queen's Head remaining. On this small site stood some 60 cottages. The area was not too desirable; that particular part of the Stourbridge Road (occupied by the word 'Street' on the enlarged section of the 1886 OS map shown over the page) was known as Rotten Row because of the hides from the tannery there which were scoured and cleaned in the Spadesbourne Brook. The stench must have been awful, but at least it was handy for the workhouse which until 1838 stood on the site of the present-day firm of solicitors (Thomas Horton & Sons).

And there were yet more nailers' cottages in the town: some in Birmingham Road, built in the early nineteenth century; a long row of over twenty in Windsor Street behind the eastern side of the High Street (by far the best since they each had the priceless asset of a long garden); another long row at Bewell Head up the Stourbridge Road, nicknamed 'the Barracks' because of their distinctly unadorned look; and a great number in the Worcester Street area, perhaps the poorest end of the town, certainly the most unhealthy because as the Spadesbourne flowed south-west through Bromsgrove it gathered the sewage and rubbish which the inhabitants of Rotten Row and the High Street saw fit to dispose of directly into the Brook.

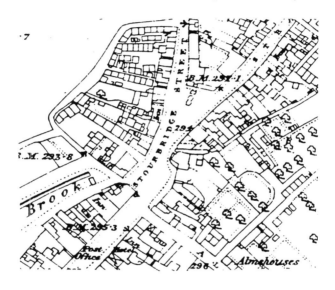

In Sidemoor, Catshill, Fairfield, Rubery, Belbroughton, Bournheath, Lickey End and Stoney Hill there were similar tiny cottages, in singles, pairs and rows with their nailshops at the side or rear, so depressingly similar, especially in the town, they might have been stamped out by a press. Many were hurriedly erected, with the bare minimum of facilities, in the late eighteenth and early nineteenth centuries when high demand for nails and the increasing popularity of an easily picked-up trade in an area of few opportunities was accompanied by a comparable demand for nailmaking facilities.

A great many of the cottages were let at a weekly rent from between 2/- and 3/- and it is clear from the 1914 Bromsgrove Valuation List that quite a number of these were owned by a comparatively few men. The long row in Windsor Street was jointly owned by Angelo Giles and John Green, while the descendants of the nineteenth-century nail manufacturer, Thomas Scroxton, owned a lot of cottages in Providence Road and in Parkside. Only when owned and let in quantity did the cottage represent a good investment.

Notices of two interesting sales of nailers' cottages are reproduced below. The first was for nine cottages and nailshops in School Lane which no longer exists but which used to be a 'pudding bag' off Worcester Road with a footpath leading across Bromsgrove School's grounds to Ednall Lane. The

---

Very Desirable FREEHOLD and Long Leasehold

PROPERTIES,

IN HIGH ST., WORCESTER ST., & CHURCH ST.,
BROMSGROVE.

MR. COTTON

HAS been favoured with instructions from the Trustees of the Bromsgrove Baptist Charities, TO SELL BY AUCTION, at the BELL INN, BROMSGROVE, on MONDAY, MAY 7th, 1883, at Five for Six o'clock in the Evening precisely, subject to Conditions then to be read, and in the following Lots :—

LOT 1.—All those

9 BRICK-BUILT AND TILED COTTAGES,

Occupying an important position at the junction of School Lane with Worcester Street, and now in the occupation of Messrs. Smith, Griffin, Byng, Whitehouse, Hemming, Perry, Troth, and Mrs. Susan Hurst, together with the Nailshops, necessary Outoffices and Land in the rear, the area of the whole being 870 Square Yards or thereabouts.— This Property, which is well supplied with water, produces a rental of £43 6s. per annum.—A small portion of this Lot is Leasehold for a term of 1000 years, from February 23rd, 1626, of which about 743 years are unexpired, at an annual rental of 15s., which sum has not been claimed for years.

'des res' description applied presumably to the investment the cottages represented rather than any intrinsically attractive features. The cottages fetched £400, an average of just under £45 each. To a nailer earning up to 15/- a week £45 should have seemed eminently affordable, equivalent to only a year's wages compared to our own day and age when many people own houses worth five, six or more times their annual income. The real point, however, is that nailers never had any surplus. It would have made little difference had the cottages been half the price, they would still have been unable to afford them, so completely trapped were they in poverty and debt.

In the 1917 sale the two nailmakers' cottages described in Lot 3 fetched between them £215, a handsome price. But they were clearly roomier than most and the large gardens would no doubt have increased the price. Sales like these marked the beginning of the end of a long era, for gradually nailmakers' cottages were being lived in by non-nailmakers, altered beyond all recognition or knocked down altogether. The most obvious physical evidence of the town's staple trade was beginning to disappear.

```
        TUESDAY,  MAY  15TH,  1917.


ESTATES OF MR. WILLIAM AND MRS. MARY COURT,
    DECEASED,  AND  MR.  E.  B.  HAZLEWOOD,
    DECEASED.


ELEVEN   FREEHOLD   COTTAGES   AT
          LICKEY END,

    FOUR  AT  CATSHILL,  AND  TWO  AT
             LYDIATE ASH,

       NORTH  BROMSGROVE.

            SMITH AND RUSSON
A   RE instructed to SELL BY AUCTION at
      THE FOREST HOTEL, LICKEY END, on
TUESDAY, MAY 15th, 1917, at Seven o'clock in
the evening punctually, subject to Conditions then
to be read the under-mentioned desirable Freehold
Properties :—
```

The trade was dying and as the century drew to a close the town in general seemed keen to get on with burial arrangements. Houses began to be built with deeds specifically prohibiting the owners from erecting nailshops. Nailers' cottages carried a stigma and the more desirable houses were not to be tainted by the old trade.

The price of nailers' cottages hardly increased with the years. In 1930 a cottage on Stourbridge Road was sold for £70, while Mrs Ethel Parsons (see Chapter Nine) remembers the cottage opposite the Crown at Catshill being sold a few years earlier for £50 to a spiritualist named Jelfs. In late 1988, when talking about the latter sale, a good-looking octogenarian in Catshill claimed that his father had bought three cottages at the turn of the century for 'ninety quid and a side of byaircon'.

Like the trade itself, many nailers' cottages stood almost unaltered from the day they were built until the day they were knocked down. Each cottage had a front door opening into a small living room, a pantry which was invariably under the stairs and at the top of the stairs a little landing and a bedroom. The earthen floor was mostly quarried and the living room was dominated by the fire and hob, with a fender which became a feature as its composition and shape grew more and more varied.

The living room furniture normally comprised a sofa, some chairs and a table. A chest of drawers was a luxury but also an obstacle as it limited the number of children who could assemble at any one time. In bad times the furniture tended to disappear in order to make ends meet. The pantry was just large enough for a couple of shelves and a sink with a single tap. A bucket on the floor supplemented the lavatory at the bottom of the yard or top of the garden; and a tin bath usually hung on a nail for the weekly dip. This was a real chore for large families—and there were some very large ones. Mrs Ivy Elvins of Broad Street (daughter of Charlie Troth; see Chapter Nine) remembers a family in York Road, Sidemoor, who had twenty-two children. Not many were quite as large but the reports of the Factory Inspectorate in the nineteenth century make it clear that nailers very often married young and had large families. According to Levett Nokes marriage in the *early* teens was not unusual:

> There are several men and their wives in the parish of Bromsgrove who, when married, were only thirty years old each couple, and they began life in poverty and will end it the same.[2]

Conversations with old nailers and their families suggest that the only items normally to be found on the pantry shelf were tea, sugar, bread and scrape, the latter a kind of margarine, dripping or lard. There was always a block of salt, though, about 10 inches square and 15 inches long, which at least added a bit of taste to what was going. Sunday was normally the only day when the fare included meat but some families managed to keep a pig and once the animal was slaughtered hung the sides of bacon from hooks in the ceiling.

At the top of the stairs the landing, just big enough for a single-sized shakedown or mattress, served to sleep two people. The bedroom could accommodate one-and-a-half beds or shakedowns. In the 1920s there were sixteen children sleeping head to toe in the bedroom of a cottage in Churchfields. Not surprizingly, the mother slept on the sofa downstairs while the father made do with a chair. Around the same time some of the children of a family in Parkside were reduced to sleeping in the shed at the bottom of the yard. My father's family consisted of six boys and four girls as well as my grandma and grandad. They lived down the Pleck in Sidemoor, but they were lucky because their cottage had two real bedrooms.

At night it was usual for the children to leave their clothes in one big pile at the bottom of the stairs. In the morning mother would call them with the cry, 'Up first, best dressed' and there would be a rush downstairs to get the best bits of clothing.

A picture of the mid-nineteenth century conditions in which the nailers lived can be gleaned from the 1851 census returns.

49 St John Street

Name	Relationship	Male	Age Female	Occupation
EADES Elizabeth	Head—Widow		(No age given)	Nailer
EADES Mary	Daughter—Unmarried		25	Nailer
EADES Edith	Daughter—Unmarried		18	Nailer
EADES Thomas	Son—Unmarried	16		Nailer
EADES Josh	Son—Unmarried	12		Nailer
EADES Oliver	Grandson	5		
EADES Josh	Grandson	4 m.		
TEDSTONE William	Lodger	17		Nailer

Here we have eight people spread across three generations and including one lodger. Six are nailers but what were their sleeping arrangements?

The family next door but two poses a similar question.

43 St John Street

Name	Relationship	Male	Age Female	Occupation
KIMBERLEY Sarah	Head—Unmarried		46	Nailer
KIMBERLEY Katharine	Daughter—Unmarried		No	Nailer
KIMBERLEY Ann	Daughter—Unmarried		ages	Nailer
KIMBERLEY Emma	Daughter—Unmarried		given	Nailer
KIMBERLEY Elizabeth	Granddaughter		4	
KIMBERLEY Edwin	Grandson	2		
CARTER Henry	Lodger	24		Nailer

This latter extract highlights another feature of nailing life which was for a long time a puzzle: why were so many heads of families unmarried? A probable answer came in the form of a question from an old friend.* 'Do you know how much a marriage licence cost in 1851? 1861? The same as it cost one hundred years later, 7/6.' In other words, nearly a week's wages for many a poor nailer. There was a tradition, according to the same friend, that in the last century on Easter Mondays the vicar of St John's would wed people free of charge, the queue stretching along St John Street and into the Kidderminster Road! Some support for this tradition comes from the activities of the vicar of Rock, beyond Stourport, who conducted marriage ceremonies free of charge in order to encourage the very poor to live in lawful wedlock.

Over the road in St John Street things are much the same.

44 St John Street

Name	Relationship	Age Male	Age Female	Occupation
JONES James	Head—Married	36		Nailer
JONES Hannah	Wife—Married		39	Charwoman
JAMES Elizabeth	Daughter-in-Law—Unmarried		No ages given	Charwoman
JAMES Mary	Daughter-in-Law—Unmarried			Nailer
JONES Matthew	Grandson	3		
JONES George	Grandson	9 m.		
INGRAM Sarah	Visitor—Married		65	Pauper
WARDELL James	Lodger—Unmarried	20		Nailer

46 St John Street

Name	Relationship	Age Male	Age Female	Occupation
EADES Mary	Head—Widow		68	Pauper
TREADWELL Pamala	Lodger—Unmarried		55	Nailer

If Mary Eades had poor law relief it would have been 3/- a week; the rent would have accounted for at least 2/- of this.

At this point it is worth looking back at the other side of the street, on the market side, where one of the other half of the nailmaking equation was living (prior to moving into a splendid house round in Kidderminster

*Fred Edmunds, well known Bromsgrove nonagenarian.

Road). Two servants were looking after the master and his small daughter.

15 St John Street

Name	Relationship	Age Male	Age Female	Occupation
SCROXTON Thomas	Head—Widower	40		Nail Manufacturer
SCROXTON Lucy	Daughter—Unmarried		2	—
HARVEY Elizabeth	Unmarried		35	Housekeeper
SEAL Mary	Unmarried		18	Servant

On the 1881 OS map about one hundred nail cottages in Bournheath are detectable, each surrounded by a piece of land varying in size from ¼ to 1½ acres. Two centuries earlier, according to Leadbetter, the area had 1000 acres of unenclosed land.[3] (Fairfield Road was always called 'The Common' by locals as is Broad Street to this day.) But it is clear from a charge made in 1797 by the Bailiff of Bromsgrove, William Blackford, that the land had been encroached upon in the previous two decades.[4] From the timing of this encroachment, and the fact that a number of Bournheath families had Catshill origins, it would appear that the search by nailers for a small piece of land to better their lot led them to Bournheath.

Other outlying areas such as Belbroughton, Fairfield, Wildmoor, Lickey End, Catshill and Sidemoor had sufficient land for most of the tiny cottages to have a garden which would be classed as 'magnificent' by today's estate agents; and it is very interesting—though not surprizing—to note how some of these traditional nailmaking areas turned more and more to growing food for a living. It is clear from the trade directories that by the end of the last century nailmaking had given way in Catshill, Bournheath and Lickey, for example, to market gardening which was being carried on extensively and profitably by former nailers.

In many agricultural districts, especially around Bromsgrove, there was the tendency for nailers to farm in the summer and leave nailmaking for the winter. Alternatives—for the town, as well—were haymaking or hop picking in Herefordshire while child nailmakers in the district would work in the fields, weeding and strawberry picking. Bromsgrove nailers, it seems, were known for their strawberry growing.

But nailing with farming or horticulture as a second string had its disadvantages. Bromsgrove specialized in hob nails, a seasonal demand since requirements of manufacturers were high during the summer and autumn (for winter stocking) but fell away in the winter months when nailers most wanted to work in their nailshops. In the 1888 Report of the Select Committee on Sweating a Catshill nailmaster is quoted as saying:

> Fully half of the men in our district are independent of the nail trade in the Summer, and they will not make them at any price . . . Most of these men have allotments of their own, and are engaged in strawberry growing, raspberry growing, and all that class of work. It takes them fully half their time to attend to these allotments of their own during the Summer months, and during those months is just the time when we could employ them best; but we cannot get them.

It wasn't a problem peculiar to Bromsgrove. The same situation held in other rural parts of the West Midlands, prompting a Quaker merchant to explain to an American customer: 'Our nailers are so much out in harvest time.'[5]

The court-dwelling nailers of Bromsgrove had no such summer alternative. Their purpose-built cottages gave no scope for growing anything. But the townie nailers did not allow the lack of gardens to dent their husbandry ambitions as Levett Nokes reveals when describing a typical Bromsgrove-court nailer of 100 years ago:

> . . . rabbits, pigeons and fowls, (which) roost and sit in the shop, and there are some who have them to sit in the home, and the moment the door is open they are in like a swarm of bees, to look after the crumbs, which makes the place look more like an out-house in a farmyard than a home. In the summer time the keeping of fowls is part of a great many nail-makers' living, as they sit the hens on duck-eggs, and keep the ducks, when they are hatched, from fourteen to twenty-eight days, and sometimes there is one hundred or more to be stored in the house and shop, besides the fowl sitting still on, as it generally lasts four or five months in the year.[6]

Hanover Street at the turn of the century. The nailshops
were at the rear of these cottages

The lot of the nailmakers was grim indeed. For most of their history
nailers were poor, working long hours for low pay in bad conditions.
Mention has already been made of the Bills of 1604 and 1621 which referred
to the poor conditions of the nailers and the abuses widespread in their
trade. In 1655 John Sanders of Harborne, a former ironmonger turned Fifth
Monarchy man and prophet, wrote one of the many pamphlets of the period,
An Iron Rod for the Naylors and Tradesmen ne'er Birmingham, urging the
masters and dealers to pay better rates to the 'poor workmen . . . many
hundreds of them enjoying nothing but misery and want'.

Debt which played such a large part in the life of the nineteenth-century
nailer had its origins in much earlier times. The fairly widespread theft
of materials from nailmasters, despite harsh penalties, was understandable
if not excusable given such awful conditions. As the nineteenth century
wore on the scandalous state of the nailing population earned the increasing
attention of Parliament and some well-placed individuals.

The situation was especially bad in the early years of the nineteenth century
when the Napoleonic Wars led to the loss of trade with America. There
was a lot of hardship and a lot of laying off—between a quarter and a third
in 1812—and those kept on were often on reduced rates. At that stage,
according to Thomas Atwood, a Birmingham banker associated with the

trade, in evidence to a House of Commons Select Committee in 1812, men were working from 4 o'clock in the morning to 10 o'clock at night for 10/- or 12/- per week. 12—14 hours had long been a normal day but as things worsened more hours had to be put in.

Another feature of the nailer's reputation, however, was his irregular approach to work: a spell of amazingly long hours would be followed by a period of idleness. Even so, it was generally accepted that in overall terms the hours worked were very long. Before the same House of Commons Committee mentioned above a nail ironmonger from West Bromwich, William Whitehouse, reckoned that the usual hours were from 5 or 6 o'clock in the morning to 11 or 12 o'clock at night for an average of 12/- a week (though many he knew earned less than 8/-). This was real poverty but it didn't prevent the ironmongers from getting together to reduce the price of nails by between 7½% and 10%.

Probably in despair some nailers at this point took themselves off to the army while others sank into the workhouse. Wages were 'so low', complained a man called Potts, 'that a man can scarcely exist'.[7] The tragedy was that life never got any better for nailers. On 18 September 1869 a lengthy description of a visit to the Black Country during a long strike appeared in The Illustrated Midland News:

> . . . the melancholy spectacle which greeted me as I stepped over the threshold of George Parson's poor dwelling, in 'Baker's Fold', was only too real . . . In the lower room sat Parson's wife sewing. Their daughter, who appeared to be about 15, was sitting by the grate, huddled up in an old shawl, nothing else. The youngest child, about four years old, was playing about the room. 'Look at her, poor dear, with hardly a bit of shoe-leather to her feet.' To detail everything in the room were a light task: one round table, with a small basin on it; some poor tattered clothes, hung up to dry; a pannikin on the hob, a tea-pot and one or two cups, a rough wooden couch, destitute of covering; this was all. The mortar showed through the bare walls.

There followed an equally harrowing description of the Parsons' bedroom:

> It contains a rough four-post bedstead, with bare poles, battered sacking, one miserable sheet, and a bolster of the

utmost attenuation. There is a 'shakedown'—a flock mattress, with no sheets, blankets, or bed-covering whatever, if you except a dirty sheet, about the size of a man's pocket-handkerchief, and so tattered and torn as to be useless for purposes of covering. There is an empty grate, that is all. In this wretched 15 by 9 room five persons sleep nightly— the father, mother and three children, aged respectively, 20 (son), 15, and 'nearly 4'. One child, 10 months old, they have buried since the strike... The brutes in the field are not more closely herded together than these unfortunate nailers. Their poverty is something appalling in its intensity. Parsons assured me that he did not know the taste of meat. They mostly had a cup of tea and some bread for breakfast, and dinner little else.

There was a brief flurry in the trade in the early 1870s (as a result of the Franco-German War) but by 1879 wages were 30% lower than in 1876 and the trade was in precipitous decline. Trade with America had declined, Belgian competition was making itself felt and improved machinery enabled cut nails to be made more cheaply.

Nailers in the Bromsgrove and Catshill district were reported to be on starvation wages;[8] and Levett Nokes describes this poverty:

In bad times, like the present, two or three families live and sleep in the same house. The writer knew of a case, in 1879, where a young woman and her child slept in the pantry, and two families slept up-stairs; and if the bailiffs had entered at that time, the furniture would not have paid more than their expenses, because it had been sold to live on.[9]

Nokes ends his little book with a plea for the capital to be found to enable the nailers to work in factories where 'they would have regular hours of labour—begin, as other men do, at six in the morning, and leave work at six . . . It would honestly enable them to get 30s per week, and no man can keep a house with anything less . . . If the trade will not afford that, the sooner it is gone to Belgium the better.'

The overriding aim of the nailers was simple survival. Until the 1830s he could get a living of some sort by working long hours and there was still some satisfaction in being, in effect, his own boss. But once the

Former nailers' cottages: (clockwise from top) Bewell Head, The Dock, Catshill, Guild Road (off Station Street), Little Rocky Lane. (Photographs by Syd Allen and Terry O'Brien)

nailmasters began to operate *bates* survival became more difficult—and the earning power of women and children even more crucial.

A former nailmaster's house, Barley Mow Lane, Catshill

Four

Women and children: all hands to the block

If the male nailer's lot was bad, the female's was often worse. Whereas in the seventeenth century it was rare for women and children to be involved in the trade, the situation changed quite dramatically during the following hundred years.

Probably the most famous description of the woman nailer comes from William Hutton, as early as 1741. Nearing the end of his journey, from Derbyshire to Birmingham by foot, Hutton, a young innocent, still not eighteen,

> . . . wondered, in my way from Walsall to Birmingham, to see so many blacksmiths' shops; in many of them one, and sometimes two *Ladies* at work; all with smutty faces, thundering at the anvil. Struck with the novelty, I asked if the ladies in this country shod horses? but was answered, "hey are nailers".[1]

He also noted elsewhere that some of the women were 'stripped of their upper garments, and not overcharged with their lower'.

By 1785 women and children accounted for perhaps as much as one-third of the nailing labour force.[2] Whole families were working at the nailblock. It was an easy trade to pick up: with no marked ability or aptitude nails *could* be made (though the really skilled work was achieved only by those who possessed both); and as the years went on every pair of hands in the family was needed, a few more nails producing a little more money. But the social cost was very high.

When a woman nailer finished her long day's work she then had to turn to some of her many other tasks involved in keeping a home and rearing children. In 1820 a woman's life expectancy (37.3 years) was three years less than that of a man's and nearly half the children she bore failed to survive. How much more dramatic were the figures for a group near the bottom of fortune's pile is not known (though bearing in mind the old adage —

hard work and a bit of dirt hurt no man — most popular, one suspects, among the poor but honest, a small study could prove interesting). For the most part, though, the nineteenth-century woman nailer must have been doomed to a short life of hard work and frequent child-bearing.

Women and girls entered nailing because there was little else in the area for them to do, the lighter work required no special strength and it was an immediate way of adding to the family's income. The proportion of female labour increased with the demise of spinning and weaving from rural districts and small towns and there were many instances of women who made nails while their husbands were employed in other occupations.

In many trades in the nineteenth century men worked at heavier and more skilful work while women were to be found in the lighter and semi-skilled branches. In nailing districts, however, it was never so clear-cut. Women were set to make the same nails as men in some cases but at a cheaper rate, a long-running source of conflict. In Bromsgrove women tended to concentrate on making smaller common nails such as the tack, the hob and the brush nail. Certainly the lighter work was physically the most compatible. Hob nails, for example, weighed between 4 and 5 lbs per 1000, the wages for these more or less exclusively female-made products being too low to attract any men to it. Operating a treadle a minimum of 3000 times in a normal day's work making smaller nails, a woman might earn 1/1½d a day at list price for hobs, a great deal less than a man putting in the same hours.

A woman nailer at the turn of the century

In practice, however, women were often put onto heavier work and they needed some strength for operating the *oliver* which formed the nail head and weighed anything from 10lbs to ½cwt, depending on the type of nail to be made. The oliver was a large hammer operated by a treadle for making larger nails. It was brought down onto the block by banging the foot, or actually jumping, on the treadle. Operating the oliver was not only hard work but bad for women, leading to miscarriages and ruptures. Some male nailers and some reformers urged the abolition of female labour but there was strong opposition to this move in many nailing districts and the government did what governments often do—nothing (allowing those involved to come round to the idea of abolition in their own good time).

In 1888 the Sweating Commission recommended that women should operate only the very lightest olivers but the rather lofty view it took of women nailers, after hearing all the evidence, suggests the failure, in part at least, to really grasp the dire economic and social problems in the trade:

> As to the question of the effect of such work upon the health, it is contended on the one hand that women suffer severely, on the other that it is only done by strong women who are quite equal to it . . . it is beyond dispute that female workers in these trades are extremely flat-chested and the mast majority of them look pale or thin, although their arms are wiry and muscular. Many of the younger women work all day in their shops, but in the case of married women with families, much time is occupied looking after their household duties. The general rule is that the the workshop has first claim and from 10 to 12 hours per day is spent by such women at the hearth and anvil. In such cases the average earnings seldom reach a higher figure than from 2/6 to 5/- per week, so it is questionable whether the small amount gained by such women in the shop is not lost by her absence from the household. As a class, the woman in these districts is completely undomesticated and has no knowledge whatever of how to use to the best advantage the small earnings of the family.[3]

They certainly earned a pittance. George Green, the general manager of the nail manufacturing firm of Eliza Tinsley & Co, gave particulars of wages for the week ending 13 October 1888 to the Sweating Commission:

Men	14/2
Women	4/9
Youths	7/7
Girls	4/1
Young Women	6/7 [4]

Without any further information about how many hours the women worked, the real comparison must be between the wages of the men and young women, both presumably on adult full-time wages.

What the Commission seems to have overlooked is that the 'small amount' of 5/- would be one-third, even more, of the nailing family's income. On the other hand, Levett Nokes, a close observer of the trade, similarly questioned how worthwhile was the woman nailer's toil in view of the pittance she earned and the effects her absence had on the life of her family:

> . . . and how can a woman keep her house and family in order if she is in a nail shop from morning till night, alongside of her husband, and the little one (if it is a baby) put in a swing, or a penthouse if it can just walk, rolling and tumbling about until its face is black and blue; and when it has dirtied itself, the woman pops out and cleans it, and throws the dirt down just outside the shop; the fowls scratch it about and the paper blows back into the house or shop . . . In some of the houses the smell is so strong that no person but those who live in it can stand it.[5]

Levett Nokes went one step further and argued that one hundred years ago women and children were the chief evils in the trade, the former because they neglected their family and the education of their children, the latter because they made such bad nails—'so bad no man on earth could drive them'.

By 1841 one in every three nailmakers in Worcestershire was a woman. A decade on, this had increased dramatically to one in every two, a ratio which remained fairly constant for the rest of that century, as the table below (from census returns) shows.

Worcestershire Nailmakers

Year	1841	1851	1861	1871	1881	1891	1901	1911
Men	3905	5150	5040	4211	3613	2012	1140	1069
Women	2321	5150	4224	4608	3926	2141	1254	698
Total	6226	10300	9267	8819	7539	4153	2394	1767

The 30% increase in the number of men employed as nailers between 1841 and 1851 largely reflects the increase in population in the county; but the rather startling 120% increase in the number of women nailers in that same decade has much more to do with the beginning of the bates: as the list price for nails was bated so more women had to work. In the Bromsgrove district by the beginning of the century there were 964 nailers left, exactly the same number of woman as men (and a total number, incidentally, almost identical to the very first figure of 1778).

Robert Sherard summed up the plight of the late nineteenth-century woman nailer in *The White Slaves of England*, a series of articles which first appeared in Pearson's Magazine in 1896 and subsequently in book form.

SHOCKING DEATH.—An accident of a dreadful character, has occurred at Bourne Heath, near this town. On the night of Wednesday last, Mary Jones, the wife of James Jones, a nailor, was left alone in the house, and on the return of her husband, in about 20 minutes, the unfortunate woman (who, it appears had been subject to fits) was found lying across the grate with her bosom on the fire; her clothes were entirely burnt off, and her body was completely charred. The husband endeavoured to force the body from the grate, but could not do so, as, either from the convulsive grasp of the deceased, or her arms being entangled between the bars, he could not remove the body till the grate was pulled down. The deceased was aged about 53, and was the mother of nine children. On Friday an inquest was held at the Crown Inn, Catshill, before Ralph Docker, Esq., and a respectable Jury when, evidence having been given of the above facts, a verdict of "Accidental Death" was returned.

From *Berrow's Worcester Journal*, 29 November 1849

Sherard, the great grandson of William Wordsworth, wrote about seven groups of workers whom he considered to be in the poorest trades in England, visiting Bromsgrove and other centres in the spring of 1896 and avoiding contact with any of the masters. Sherard had a strong social conscience which led him here and there to interpret situations in terms more black-and-white than they probably were (as he did, for example, when describing nailmasters). Even so, one cannot help but be moved by some of the descriptions recorded. 'I has been married twenty-three years' said one woman, who had reared six children and was still working a nine-hour day for 1/-, 'and I has never had a new dress since I were married.' Tea, bread and margarine were the staple food, bread and cheese an occasional treat and 'sixpenny worth of meat came once a week' with a bit of luck. 'Amusement?' she added. 'There is none for me; bed and work is all we get.'

Another, a mother of two surviving children, said that by Sunday, when all debts had been paid, she was left with nothing to 'go to town with and buy a bit of meat for Sunday's boiling'. She had had only two new dresses since her marriage sixteen years before, one of these the result of 'a subscription which was raised at her chapel, when she buried her eldest child and a black dress seemed necessary'.

One of the bits of evidence Sherard took away with him from Bromsgrove was a written account of how a nailing couple, both in the trade, and their five children managed on 15/- a week:

	s	d			s	d
Rent	2	6	Cheese			5
Firing	1	6	Sugar			7
Repair of tools & kitchen fuel	1	6	Tea			4½
			Tobacco			3
Bread	4	6	Lamp oil			2
Bacon		9¾	Candles			1¼
Meat		9	Soap			3
Margarine	1	0	Sundries			3½

Meat, potatoes, medicines and clothing must have been just a few of the items described as sundries.

Remaining in Sherard's head after he left the town was the voice of an old lady, bowed and almost blind, singing with enthusiasm, hope and fervour 'The Lord will provide'.

A deplorable aspect of nineteenth-century industrial life was the employment of children, a practice which continued in the nailshops for most of the century despite a series of reforming Acts aimed at raising their entry age, shortening working hours and encouraging school attendance. In Worcestershire the middle decades saw a positive explosion of young people employed in nailing.

Young Nailmakers of Worcestershire

	1841	1851	1861	% Increase
No. of males employed under age of 20	871	1545	2057	136
No. of females employed under age of 20	399	1429	2162	442

From: Censuses of Production

The increase in the number of young females during this period is astounding. In no other area in the country do we find such figures. A more detailed breakdown of the 1861 census for Worcestershire and Staffordshire is even more startling, especially when compared with the overall figure for England and Wales.

	U5	5	10	15	20	25	35	45	55	65	75	85	Total
England & Wales— Males	170	1559	1714	1529	2527	2431	2256	1707	977	385	66	0	15,321
— Females	150	1668	2211	1665	1942	1377	883	513	175	63	10	0	10,657
Staffordshire — Males	43	380	383	281	536	486	497	364	232	57	1	0	3,260
— Females	77	870	1247	883	967	753	469	291	156	27	1	0	5,741
Worcestershire — Males	95	710	662	590	908	732	618	437	211	70	7	0	5,040
— Females	69	712	767	614	825	540	362	195	108	28	1	0	4,221

From: 1861 Census

The fact that in Worcestershire alone 164 children (95 boys and 69 girls) under the age of five and 1422 (710 boys, 712 girls) between five and ten years of age were defined as nailers by occupation is staggering. The under-20s constituted no less than one-third of the labour force.

In giving evidence to the Children's Employment Commission in 1862 one nailmaker is quoted as saying:

I should not like my little boy there, now 5, to begin before 9, and he shan't be if I can help it, but if I am always obligated, I must. He is but a little mossel and if I were to get that little creature to work, I would have to get a scaffold for him to stand on to reach, and with that it would be like murder-work as you might say.

The nailer's child knew all about nailshops, making his first appearance there as a tiny baby in a clothes basket or other container. This was placed conveniently on the bellows so that every time they were pumped the baby was rocked, perhaps to

> Jeremiah, blow the fire
> Puff-puff-puff

or one of the many other nailing songs or hymns which helped to relieve the boredom.

From the moment he was judged to be of some use the child became a bellows blower, standing on a box to reach the handle. By anticipating the completion of the nails by the nailer and having the irons in the fire ready for him, a few seconds could be saved on each nail. He had to be ready for work, however, as soon as his mother and father so that the hours for all were terribly long. Many children stood in the roof with their backs against a beam and pumped the bellows with their feet. When more than one nailer worked in the shop the child would pump two bellows in sequence, anticipating the completion of the nail on each of the two blocks. Only straightforward anatomy saved him from having to blow for more than two nailers.

The nailblock itself was too high for a very young child to look down on but as soon as he was able he was set to work; and on the day he made his first saleable nail he was given a penny dated for that year. It was often kept for the whole of his life and shown with some pride to his friends. But that same penny in effect chained the boy to the nailblock for life. And some older people in the Bromsgrove area remember another, much more cruel, custom. In a horribly appropriate way, the reuluctant young nailer would be nailed to the doorpost through the lobe of his ear until he agreed to start — or resume — work.

Inhumanly long hours took their toll on the children:

> This accounts for many of them (the great majority) being stunted and delicate and having faces appearing many years older than their bodies.[6]

The layout of the nailshop also led to a high incidence of death by burning. In 1838 in Sedgley alone ten children were burned to death.[7] And just as tragic was the effect of some quack cordials given to the younger children to keep them quiet while mother worked. Godfrey's Cordial was one of these, widely advertized in the papers of the day, a mixture of boiled treacle, water and opium. It was probably ignorance about what happened to this Victorian sedative when left standing in a very hot workshop that accounted for a number of infant deaths.

If the child was not busy in the workshop the chances were he or she would be nursing the baby of the family, or someone else's baby for 1/- a week. It would be reasonable to assume that the employment of factory inspectors from the early years of the nineteenth century would have helped protect young children from the worst conditions and abuses of working life. For many decades, however, attention was only given to those working in factories and mines, not workshops. The series of factory acts, aimed at regulating conditions of employment, only gradually improved things for children and for many years had no effect at all on cottage industries like nailing (nor on a number of non-cottage industries): children and adults continued to work long hours in the lean-to nailshop in the most squalid conditions, oblivious of the finer things in life and for the most part unable to read or write.

The very nature of cottage industries made improvement difficult. In all the domestic trades it was natural before the days of compulsory education — and after — for children to help their parents. (Child labourers were not confined to the cottage, though, for it seemed just as 'natural' to society to let them work in factories, go up chimneys and clean streets.) In both domestic workshops and factories there was a distinct tendency for men and women to work irregular hours, often attempting a week's work in just three or four days. This was particularly prevalent among nailers, as the Report of the Inspectors of Factories for April 1874, for example, shows; and it meant that, as young children had to blow the bellows when their parents worked, they too worked long hours, often in the second half of the week. Society as a whole — including, it has to be said, many nailers themselves—simply did not feel strongly enough about their plight. It is probably true to say that the trade died before it was reformed.

Hand-wrought nailing was not governed by the series of factory acts passed in the middle decades of the nineteenth century; but there were great hopes following the appointment of the Children's Employment Commission in 1862 for on this occasion both chainmaking and nailmaking were to be considered. The report was finished in 1864 but despite its very important position in the trade Bromsgrove was not among the areas of North Worcestershire chosen by members of the Commission to visit. However, one of the report's many comments about the poor state of the nail trade in general would certainly have applied to the Bromsgrove area:

> Many of the men work all hours—their labour being bounded by the limits of physical endurance, *eg* till a man can hardly reach up to the door or put one foot before the other. Their children share with them, as far as their physical powers endure, in the exhausting labour.

The following two examples of *depositions*, summaries of statements made by children before the Commission in 1862/3, give a good picture of the lot of the child nailer everywhere.

Deposition No 390: Richard Nock Aged 10

Works at nailing with his father, mother, sisters and brothers, not all in the same shop; his sisters work in nail-shops in Wales; gets up to work in the morning about 4 o'clock and leaves off at 8 at night, with half an hour for breakfast, an hour for dinner, and half an hour for tea; they get enough to eat; they all work Monday; can read in the Testament; went to a day school when he was three years old, and was taken away at four years old to work at nails.

Further comments on this boy revealed that the Commission considered him to be well grown, tolerably clean and well clothed, but unhealthy and with sore eyes.

Deposition No 397: Mary Ann Perry Aged 9

Works at nailing with her mother, her grandfather and her grandmother, her uncle Jonah and her aunt Elizabeth. They all go to work at six in the morning, have their breakfast at nine for half an hour; work on till one o'clock, then go to their dinners till two; then work again till five, have half an hour for tea, then they all go to work again till nine. They don't laugh over their work, very seldom, hardly ever, have no time to laugh. She laughs herself sometimes but aunt Elizabeth laughs most. Can read—reads about God and all, in a little spelling book.

The Commission's additional comments on Mary were happy ones compared to many: she was healthy, clean, well clothed and very intelligent. But clearly from their pursuit of the subject, at least some Commission members were worried about a trade which gave rise to such little laughter.

It wasn't until 1867 that legislation included in its sphere those employed in workshops. Under the Workshops Regulation Act children between eight and thirteen were to attend school for ten hours a week and work for no more than thirty; and young people and women were prevented from working more than ten-and-a-half hours a day and those only between 5am and 9 pm. Following on this the Report of the Inspectors of Factories in October 1868 must have given rise to some hope amongst those interested in the welfare of the children of Bromsgrove:

> An Inspector of Workshops who is himself a working nailer has been appointed, with a salary jointly paid to him by the township of Bromsgrove and the outlying district of Catshill; and the committee and managers of the national schools have decided, for the present, to open an afternoon school for boys at the Town-Hall Bromsgrove, and for girls at the girls' Schoolroom at Catshill . . . an attendance of at least 350 children from the workshops in the district is expected.

The expectation was wildly optimistic. Only 46 children turned up. At the same time the inspector Joshua Steele — local though he was, appropriately experienced though he was—had a district to cover which included the Putcheon (the area behind the Stourbridge Road between Meadows First School and the Hundred House, a maize of nailers' cottages), Sidemoor, Catshill, Little Catshill, Lickey End, The Whetty (which stretched from Spring Pools, near Lydiate Ash, to the top of Rubery where there was a little nailmaking centre, a few cottages still in evidence), Dodford, Belbroughton, Staple Hill, Alfred's Well, Stoke and Droitwich. It was a pretty hopeless task and after less than five years the post was abandoned. Yet a letter to the Factories Inspector from the Vicar of Catshill, Rev James Kidd, makes it abundantly clear why the district should have persevered with a local inspection system. Among the individual cases described by the clergyman, and quoted in the Inspectors of Factories Report of November 1872, is the following harrowing description of a young boy:

> E F is a drunken fellow with a wife and five children. The

mother and eldest girl and a boy have often worked early and late, and will do so again—at least two of them will. The boy, poor fellow, is dead. He was taken ill on a Friday and died the following Friday. Even during his illness he could take no food, and was almost too weak to stand. His father compelled him to work up till the Monday. He was eleven years old but so weak and emaciated. He could earn 4/- a week.

The inspectors themselves were still complaining over a quarter of a century later that there were too few of them to be able to ensure that children attended school and were treated properly. In the Report of the Royal Commission on Labour of 1892 a nail official is quoted as saying that he could not recall seeing a factory inspector in the Bromsgrove area for over ten years and this had proved very bad for the children.

Those who did manage to get to school for ten hours often had to get up much earlier to cram in the same amount of nailing; and many were 'encouraged' by parents to get the ten hours over as soon as possible, that is, in the first two days—a very unsatisfactory approach to their bit of schooling.

When commitment to a local inspector petered out the district was left to the care of the Factory Inspector responsible for the nail and chain districts of the whole of the Black Country. In a report of 1875 he quotes Mr Dodd, headmaster at the National School in Crown Close:

On Books   1873— 4
              1874—71
              1875—81

Attendance well sustained. General willingness to conform to regulations. The majority of boys show deplorable ignorance, for 8 cases out of 10 are unable to do anything but read, and this very elementary. A steady attendance for 12 months might, with very hard work, bring 25 per cent of them up to second standard.

It was a dramatic increase in attendance from the four souls in 1873 to the 71 in 1874; but still, comparatively, only a handful when the population of over 10,000 is borne in mind.

In the previous year, 1874, the master at Catshill National School had reported a similarly sad state of affairs:

> The number of workshop children in attendance is 53 . . .
> Trade being good, many children are taken away from
> nursing and put to the nail block. By far the greater part
> of these have never attended a school. Of the 68 half-timers,
> 28 are in the lower standard. In fact every half-timer has
> to be sent into the lowest division of the last class, being
> literally only fit for a low class in the infant room.

But there were people in society at large who were growing increasingly
sympathetic towards children—and women—and increasingly concerned
about the plight of child labourers and their lack of education. And some

> 5th. February 1877   A great decrease in the
> number of children owing to the Strike in the nail
> trade, the parents not being able to pay the school
> fees.
>
> 5th. March 1877   A very full school owing to the
> Managers having decided to allow the children a
> free admittance during the strike.
>
> 1 July 1881   The nailers being on strike, very few
> children present.
>
> 18th. August 1881   It has been decided to remit
> the fees of all Nailers children for the purpose of
> ensuring a better attendance in the school.

From the log books of Sidemoor School, Bromsgrove.

of the nailers themselves were at last starting to change their attitude. In
1869 the nailmasters agreed among themselves to bate prices once more.
The new list they issued, showing a 10% bate, became known as the
'starvation list'. From then onwards nailers agreed 'it was a crime to teach
a lad', ie the nailing trade. Census figures show that in the ten years between
1861 and 1871 the number of boy nailers in Worcestershire under 20 years
of age fell from 2057 to 478. This growing determination to prevent their
children from entering the nail trade stemmed not so much from lofty views

about the intrinsic importance of childhood as from conviction that there was nothing that could be said in the trade's favour: it remained badly paid, badly organized, unhealthy and without a future.

But the widespread neglect and ill-usage of children was a long time dying. Even the 1870 Education Act making school attendance compulsory took time to bite. Children and parents lied about their age and made excuses about sickness, as Levett Nokes makes clear:

> In March 1883, a man had a daughter who had begun to nail, and neglected to go to school; so the School Attendance Officer went to know how it was. "O", the father's reply was, "her's begun to try to make nails." The School Attendance Officer said she had better go to school, or else the father would be summoned. The man said she should be sure to go next Monday. When Monday came, he said to himself, "I have a payment to make this week, so she must stop and help to get that," and the following Monday she went to school. As soon as the teacher saw her, she said, "Mary Ann, your name is scratched off"; and when her father heard it, he said that was just what he wanted to hear; so the girl, as far as learning is concerned, is ruined for life, and no doubt, when a woman, will curse the School Board for allowing her guardians to keep her without education.[8]

The most common plea for non-attendance was: 'I want them to nurse the baby at home', which in practice meant sneaking them into the nailshop.

Attitudes to education were changing however. A number of local schools have celebrated their centenary and from the log books of one of these, Sidemoor First School, built in 1864 on a piece of land given by the Earl of Plymouth, these changes can be seen:

> 17th January 1874
> Reopened school after Christmas vacation, 54 children present
> 5th February 1877
> A great decrease in the number of children owing to the Strike in the Nail Trade, the parents not being able to pay the school fees
> 5th March 1877
> A very full school owing to the managers having decided to allow the children free admission during the strike

References in the log books of Meadows First and Fairfield First Schools show similar important changes of attitude. Children were at last being given a chance to get on the road out of nailing and the educators (in Bromsgrove, at least) were prepared to encourage this by remitting the school fees for a time—a real revolution in thought. By 1911 (the last census to record nailers as a separate group) only 35 children under 15 years of age were working as nailers in the Bromsgrove area.

Hob nails, usually made by women
(Photograph by Terry O'Brien)

In June 1846 Elihu Burritt, citizen of the USA (and later to return to England as his country's consul in Birmingham) set out from Edgbaston on a walking tour and headed south-west:

A mile or two further on towards Bromsgrove (Lickey) I was caught in a shower, and turned into a nalier's shop by the road-side for shelter. It was not much larger than a good-sized potato bin with a tile roof to it. Here a father and his son were busily at work. The lad was only nine years old, standing with bare feet on a stone to raise him breast-high to the anvil. His face was smutty of course, as it ought to have been, and his long black hair was coarse and unkempt. He could not read, nor could his father afford to send him to school . . . and not dreaming that any younger or poorer was to be found at the same work, I made a little martyr of him in my own mind, and wrote my impressions of his condition in an article which had a wide reading in the United States. It excited so much sympathy that, at my suggestion, the

American children raised a contribution of about £30 to send him to school, and to pay his father 2/6d a week in lieu of his wages. When he grew to be of age, he came to me in New England and worked a year on my farm; and is still living in my native town, the father of several happy children.[9]

At least one boy nailer got a very lucky break.

Invoice of 1910 from William Mason, nail manufacturer, to Thomas Appleby, High Street ironmonger, for three gross of frost nails.

Five

Doing your stint: working the iron

> I always love to walk about in the villages of the nail-makers. The clinking of hundreds of their little hammers supply the *aria* to the great concerts and oratorios of mechanical industry . . . They are poorly-paid and have to work long and hard to earn bread . . . but thousands of families have inherited the trade . . . and they are born to it, apparently with a physical conformation to the work . . . Although they earn little, they earn it at home, and the whole social operation and aspect of their industry is rather interesting . . . These little house-shops . . . really make comfortable little homes for honest and contented labourers.[1]

It is hard to believe that this uniquely romantic view from an outsider, Elihu Burritt, the American Consul in Birmingham, could have been written in a period of great discontent and on the very eve of a further cut in the price of nails, known amongst nailers as the 'starvation list'. He seems not to have noticed the widespread distress, despair and ill health of workers cooped up for hours on end in hot filthy hovels known as workshops. Just as well, perhaps, that Burritt's book was unlikely to have been read by those concerned.

Much closer to the mark—and representative of other writers' comments on the situation—is Robert Sherard's description of the nailer at work:

> The persistent labouriousness of these men was my first impression. Not for one second did they interrupt their mechanical movements, undisturbed by our advent, indifferent to all but the maximum to be effected. They answered my questions, even made comments, but their weary eyes never deflected from their work, their hands and feet busy in one monotonous jig. Now it was working the

bellows, now stoking the fire, now turning the irons and now fashioning them on the bench—a series of brusque, jerky, harassed movements, not for one second suspended; perpetual motion under the whip of hunger, as long as nerves could direct and muscles fulfil.[2]

The nailmaker's craft and workshop changed hardly at all over the centuries; and unlike those who worked in the textile industries, who for the most part moved from their domestic environment into the factories, very few nailers were absorbed into nailmaking factories. Most moved into new kinds of work when and where they arose.

The nailshop was small—often not much more than 9 foot square—and filthy, resembling, when the fire went out, a coalhole. Each was fitted with a forge and bellows and, whether it was owned or rented, the nailer had to provide his own bench and tools which cost between £5 and £10.

The bench was fitted with a small anvil on which the red-hot iron was pointed, a fixed chisel over which the iron was bent and partly cut, and a bore into which the cut length of iron was inserted prior to shaping the nail head. The shaping of the head was achieved by the use of the oliver, a heavy hammer operated by a treadle and returned to its upright position by a straightforward leverage system. A lever ejected the finished nail from the bore.

Many nailers neither rented nor owned a workshop. Instead they rented a 'stall' which in effect allowed them to heat the rod in the same fire but to make their nails independently using their own tools. In this way a lot of nailshops accommodated four nailers, each working at his own bench and anvil at one of the corners of the central hearth. The 'stallers' paid between 6d and 8d rent and an appropriate percentage of the cost of breeze (fuel).

One of the members of the Children's Employment Commission which reported in 1864, Mr E White, had this to say about the nailers' forges:

They remain as they are described to have been in the neighbourhood districts 20 years ago: small gloomy hovels adjoining the cottages with barely room for two workers, their fire and anvils unfloored, and often slightly below the level of the ground outside, and so in wet soils likely to be unhealthy from the damp ... One of these places, in which a strong man caught consumption of which he died, is

spoken of as being so wet that the water stood on the ground
and escaped by the door sill, and as having had 26 buckets
full of water taken one morning from a hole dug in the floor
to collect the moisture.

The bundles of iron supplied by the masters or foggers, usually weighing
60 lbs, were circular, square or rectangular in cross-section, depending on
the type of nail to be made. The iron rods were cut usually into three for
more convenient handling; and, since the last five or six inches could not
be used because much too hot to handle, there was a certain amount of
wastage. The nailmaster took this into account and made allowance for it
according to the type of nail. As much as 15lbs allowance was made in the
making of some small nails (for which Bromsgrove was noted) but very
much less, 3 or 4 lbs, when spikes were made. The weight of nails the master
expected back from the allocated bundles of iron rod was known as the
'yield' or 'stent' (later *stint*).

A skilled nailer could make up a little out of this wastage, hammer-welding
the fag-ends of the iron rods together to make a convenient length of iron
and selling the extra nails direct for as much as a further 1/- a week. On
the other hand, it was often not worth it for time was wasted and the rhythm
broken, a crucial factor in the mass production of the domestic nail trade.

On the very first day of his visit to Bromsgrove Robert Sherard visited
a nailshop not far from St John's Church and found there three nailers—
the tenant and two stallers—hard at work making Flemish tacks. They each
reckoned to be able to make as many as 24000 tacks in a week provided
they worked a fifteen-hour day. A tack must thus have taken no more than
a few seconds to make; and for this superhuman effort the men were earning
the princely sum of 10/10d a week.[3]

In the following illustrations the nailmaker is Albert Crane of The
Common (Broad Street), Bromsgrove who was making nails when these
photographs were taken in about 1950, a couple of years before he died.
The photographs show the six different operations involved in the making
by hand of a single nail.

1 Heating the iron in the muffle

There appears to be only one iron in the *muffle* (fire). More often there
were two, even three. All important was the *breeze,* the special fuel used
(also known as *gleeds).* Breeze consisted of small pieces of coke already used

in the puddling furnaces of the Black Country, collected and washed and resembling little bits of coke. In many areas it was hawked from door to door at 6d or 7d a three-bushel sack. In the Bromsgrove area, however, from the middle of the nineteenth century coke was bought from the Gas Works off Worcester Road and broken up into pieces about one inch in size. The muffle had to be red-hot; hence the importance of the *teasers* (bellows).

2 Drawing out the tang of the nail

Turning the heated iron rod with one hand the nailer drew out, or fashioned, the *tang* (point) by repeated hammering on a small block called the anvil, the latter a small piece of hardened steel driven into a cast iron block. Hammering gave the tang a certain hardness and durability whilst the hammer marks themselves meant the nail was more difficult to get out once it was driven in. A number of nails had tangs which were three or even four inches long. Charlie Troth, Bromsgrove's last nailmaster and maker, reckoned that one particular type of fancy Welsh nail had a tang five inches long.

1.   2.

3 Bending the nail on the hardy

The *hardy* was a fixed chisel placed vertically in the nailblock. Enough iron was left above the tang to make the *yod* (head the nail). At this stage the piece of pointed iron was bent over the hardy with a single blow of the hammer, leaving it attached only by sufficient metal to be able to be twisted off manually at the next operation.

3.   4.

4 Breaking off the nail in the bore
The tang was then inserted in the bore and the rod twisted, enabling the nail to be broken off ready for the next stage.

5 Yodding the nail with the oliver
The oliver was a heavy hammer operated by a treadle. Into it could be placed different head-shapes according to the type of nail to be made. By banging the foot on the treadle the oliver was brought down, flattening the protruding mass and shaping the head (yodding). Albert Crane is seen here with two irons making two nails simultaneously. This was not a regular achievement but first-class nailers could make two nails from two irons consecutively. (Hence the expression 'two irons in the fire')

6 Ejecting the completed nail with the paddle
The completed nail was ejected from the bore by tapping the *paddle* with a hammer which forced the ejector pin up the bore.

How much of the iron bar was heated at each blowing depended on the kind of nail being made. A good nailer could make two nails out of one heating, the very best could make three. Most however made one nail from a heat.

5.

6.

It is not too difficult to imagine the rhythm required in making a nail: heating the iron, tapping it to remove scale, swivelling round, one or two steps to the block, making the nail, swivelling again and back to the hearth, replacing the iron in the fire (and pumping the bellows if no child on hand*). It is little wonder the nailers got exasperated at any interference with this flow; and they continued in 'perpetual motion' even in the presence of Sherard who was looking for ammunition to fight their cause.

In 1933 E I Davies, author of 'The Midland Hand-Wrought Nail Trade', an unpublished thesis in Birmingham University, watched a Catshill nailer making brush nails. In full flow his record was 40 nails in five minutes—7½ seconds a nail.

*Not always an advantage! As a small boy I remember climbing onto my grandad's nailshop roof in Brighton's Yard and tipping a can of water down the 'chimmuck'. The smut rose into grandad's face as he was pumping the bellows. He grabbed one of the pieces of red-hot iron, rushed out of the nailshop and caught me just as I was sliding off the roof. I carry the scars to this day (as many Women's Institute groups will verify).

The variety of handmade nails was enormous; different areas naturally came to specialize in particular types. This meant the nailmaster could not only limit the types of iron he kept in stock but also get from his nailers a better quality nail because of specialisation.

The good nailmaker of course could make most types of nail but the most difficult nails to make, the horse-, mule- and oxshoe nails, were made only by the cream of the trade, the most skilled men (women were excluded) who operated in the Dudley area. A horseshoe nailer could earn £1 a week when others were lucky to be getting 12/-. For icy roads frost cogs and frost nails were made for mule-and horseshoes, not just in Dudley but in various places in the Black Country and in Bromsgrove.

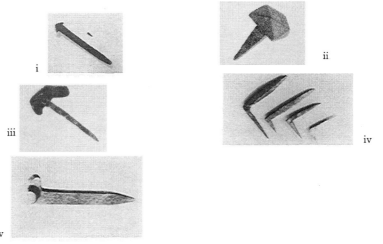

Nails galore: i. 'brob' (ship's nail) and 'sparrable'   ii. pattern for a decorative nail   iii. alpine clinker   iv. tenterhooks.   v. dog-eared spike

When certain countries operated tariffs against imported finished goods, inlcuding nails, a 'Brazil' nail was developed, a partly completed horse nail which had to be finished on arrival. Thus with a little ingenuity the restriction was overcome. Millions of these were required and two of them resided in the old oak doorpost of what used to be Latham's butcher's shop (now the jeweller's, H Samuel) in Bromsgrove High Street. Having once set out with a claw hammer to whip them out for souvenirs—only to be defeated by the King's conscience—I left them in for a throwaway remark during town walks. But the devilish demolition machine got there first.

A second category of nails was the larger nail, especially the spike and in particluar the dog-eared spike and the brob, made in the Black Country with Halesowen as the centre. A number of spikes were made for other craftsmen as their names indicate: cooper's clasp, glazier's sprig and tenterhook (the latter for holding cloth stretched on a tenter or frame).

The third main category of nails was known as small work. Bromsgrove was always noted for its smaller nails, eventually becoming the centre of this branch of the trade, turning out billions of the small common nails such as tacks, hob and brush nails. But there were also less common nails such as clinkers, tingles, battins and scuppers.

The tremendous range of handmade nails becomes evident if the hob nail is taken as an example. The different types of this nail alone included: clasp, round, patent, Welsh, square, fancy, fancy square, Albert, star, Victoria, cress, fitter, HM square, HM fitter and snap taper.

The names of the old handmade nails could justify a small dictionary. There is always a rhyme and reason for them—not, though, always quite as obvious as may appear. Below is a brief explanation of how a number of the nails made in the Bromsgrove area got their names and what they were used for.

Albert hob	Named after Prince Albert's headgear, used at the other end of the anatomy, *ie* for boots and shoes
Alpine clinker	A very difficult nail to make, this went round the climber's boots and was named after the 'clink-clink' noise thus produced. It had a very long tang and a tongue which was much exaggerated. Clinkers helped prevent climbers from slipping
Battin (or Batten)	Principally used for nailing floorboards, the shape of the nail's head enabling it to be lost below the surface of the board when hammered in. It was presumably named after the word for the long narrow boards used for flooring, *ie* battens
Brad	In earlier times called broddus or braddus, the name probably originated in the Old English word *brord* meaning 'point'. Brads were headless nails which, when driven in, could be lost below the surface
Brush	Like an enlarged tack, it held the ferrule onto the brush
Clasp	A large easily sunk nail for clasping together any two items *eg* floorboards to joists
Clout	A short flat-headed nail used particularly for attaching sheet metal to wood. Connected with the Old English

	word *clut,* a piece of metal or cloth, and/or the fourteenth-century word *clout,* to strike with the hand
Cress	So named because its head resembled the characteristic appearance of the cress family *ie* four petals arranged like a cross
Dog-eared spike	This was used for holding down railway track and was made by the billion in the great railway era. It resembled a dog's profile
Flemish tack	A light small all-purpose nail named after similar ones made in Flanders
Miner's clinker	See *alpine clinker.* This one went round the toe of the miner's boot
Sparrable	The local pronunciation of *sparrow bill,* the name self-explanatory. Sparrables were used for holding window frames prior to puttying, and also for picture frames
Strake	A cart tyre nail, also called a *stub.* Strake is the same word as that for the curved metal plate forming part of the metal rim on a wooden wheel
Tenterhook	A hook-shaped nail used for holding cloth when stretched on a tenter or wooden frame. Hence the term 'on tenterhooks'
Tingle	Similar to a tack but much sharper and finer so that when it was picked up andstuck in the finger it caused a tingling sensation

There were many other specialized nails made for specific purposes. Door nails of a decorative nature, for example, were made to order. The larger door nail in the illustration is actually a wooden pattern given to a Bromsgrove nailer for the type he had to make. The smaller door nail is one salvaged from the old Clock House building, Bournheath, when it was needlessly demolished.

For some 150 years at least the pig ring was a speciality of the Bromsgrove nailer. Though not exactly a nail millions were made by the nailers of the area, including my grandfather. I was once bragging to an old gentleman about the originality of the Bromsgrove pig ring. 'You fellows from the town don't know everything' he said with a sly grin. He took from a drawer a battered horseshoe nail which he explained had been used for ringing pigs for centuries. Not until the end of the eighteenth century, he pointed out, did the Bromsgrove pig ring appear and later still the modern wire ring. He gave me a specially made pair of pliers for fashioning the wire ring; and, finally, a twentieth-century piece of torture, a pig ring with four razor-sharp prongs which are inserted forcibly into the pig's snout with the pliers. I had been given the history of the pig ringing over several hundred years, and all for free.

Even with a maths degree a full understanding of the system of payment is almost impossible. A hundred years ago William Cotton came to the same conclusion:

> Seeing that there are very many varieties of nails, and that each variety is paid for at a different rate, it would be almost impossible to give this list; and we doubt, indeed, whether our readers would understand it if we did.[4]

And later in that same decade the Select Committee on Sweating reported:

> This is one of the oldest of trades carried on in the Midlands and price lists are still to be seen which show the prices of no less than 27 distinct classes of nails made in the district before the commencement of the present century . . . the whole system of payment for nails, whether by weight, number or tale, was so technical and complicated in 1841 as to require for its elucidation a book of tables of 132 quarto pages.[5]

Essentially, the price paid to the nailer was based on two calculations. Those who made horseshoe nails and those who made other larger sorts of nails were paid by the hundredweight and their work was known as *hundred work*. Those who made smaller nails were paid by the thousand and their work was known as *thousand work*. So far, so simple. But though one kind of work was reckoned by weight and the other by number all nails in practice were weighed, the 'thousand work' reckoned up as so many pounds weight per thousand. The prices for nails differed according to their class and variety, those in the 'common nail' trade (every kind of nail, that is, apart from horse nails) supposed to be regulated by a 'list' price.

Bromsgrove, December, 1846.

Rose and Flemish Tack

2½oz		7¼
5		7¼
6		7½
7		7¾
8		8
10		8½
12		9
14		9½
16		10
18		10½

Best and Fine Flemish.

2½		9
5		9
6		9¼
7		9½
8		9¾
9		10
10		10½
12		11
14		11½
16		12
18		12½
20		13

Fine Clout.

1¼lb	1	2¼
1½	1	3¼
2	1	4½
2¼	1	5¾
2½	1	7
2¾	1	8
3	1	9
3½	1	11
4	2	1
4½	2	2¾
5	2	4¼
5½	2	6¼
6	2	8
7	2	11½
8	3	3
9	3	6½
10	3	10

BoreTip same
Round Trunk
1½ more

Best Clout.

1¼	1	2
1½	1	3
2	1	4
2¼	1	5
2½	1	6
2¾	1	6½
3	1	7¼
3¼	1	8¼
3½	1	9¼
3¾	1	10¼
4	1	11¼
4½	2	1¼
5	2	3¼
5½	2	4½
6	2	6¼
7	2	10½
8	3	2
9	3	5
10	3	9

Com. Clout.

1¼lb	1	0¼
1½	1	1½
2	1	2½
2¼	1	4
2½	1	4½
3	1	5¼
3¼	1	6¼
3½	1	7¼
3¾	1	8½
4	1	9
4½	1	10½
5	2	0½
5½	2	2
6	2	3¾
7	2	7
8	2	10¼
9	3	2
10	3	5½

Com. Battin.

5oz		6
6		6¼
7		6½
8		7
9		7¼
10		7½
11		7¾
12		8¼
14		9
16		9½
18		10
20		10½
1¼lb		11½
1½		13
2		14
2¼		15
2½		16
3		18
3½		19
5	2	2
6	2	5¼

Fine Battin.

2½ & 3oz.		6½
5		7
6		7¼
7		7½
8		8
9		8¼
10		8½
11		8¾
12		9¼
13		9½
14		10
16		10½
18		11
20		12
1¼lb		13½
1½		14½
2	1	3½
2¼	1	4½
2½	1	5½
2¾	1	6½
3	1	7½
3¼	1	8½
3½	1	9½
3¾	1	10½
4	1	11½
4½	2	1½
5	2	3½
6	2	7

Fine Clasp.

16oz.	1	2
18	1	2½
20	1	3¼
1¼lb	1	4½
1½	1	5¼
2	1	6
2¼	1	6¾
2½	1	7½
2¾	1	8¼
3	1	9¼
3¼	1	10¼
3½	1	11
3¾	2	0
4	2	1
4½	2	2½
5	2	4
5½	2	6
6	2	7½
6½	2	9¼
7	2	11
8	3	2
9	3	5½
10	3	9

Long Clasp.

7	1¾in.	2	9
8	2 —	3	0
10	2¼—	3	6
12	2½—	4	0½
14		4	7
16		5	1
18		5	7
20		6	1
24		7	0

Cr. Sk. Clout.

4½	2	1¼
5	2	3½
5½	2	5
6	2	6½
7	2	10
9	3	5
10	3	9
11	4	0½
12	4	4
14	4	11
16	5	6
20	6	6
24	7	6
28	8	6

Larger, 33s. per cwt.

Rivets.

8oz.		8½
10		9
12		9½
14		10
16		10¼
18		10½
20		11
1¼lb		12
1½		13
2		13½
2¼	1	2¼
2½	1	3¼
2¾	1	4¼
3	1	5¼
3¼	1	6¼
3½	1	7¼
3¾	1	8
4	1	9
5	2	0
6	2	3
8	2	9

Clasp Hobs.

14oz		10
16		10¼
18		10½
20		11
1¼lb		12
1½		13
2		13½
2¼		14½
2½		15½
2¾		16½
3		17½
3¼		18½
3½	1	7½
3¾	1	8
4	1	9
4½	1	10½
5	2	0
5½	2	1½
6	2	3½
6½	2	5
7	2	6½
8	2	9½
9	3	0½
10	3	4
11	3	7½
12	3	10½

Clinkers, 2d., Fine Hobs, 1½ and Iron Tacks, ½ per m. more.

Round Heads.

8oz		9
9		9¼
10		9½
11		9¾
12		10
13		10¼
14		10½
16		11
18		11½
20	1	0
1¼lb	1	1½
1½	1	2½
2	1	3½
2¼	1	4
2½	1	5
2¾	1	6
3	1	7
3¼	1	8
3½	1	9
3¾	1	10
4	1	11
4½	2	0½
5	2	2½
6	2	5½

Tip Nails.

1¼	1	2
1½	1	3
2	1	4
2½	1	6
3	1	8
3½	1	10

Counter Horse Tip, 2d. more.

Fine Brush.

1¼	½in.	1	4½
1½	½	1	5½
2	¾	1	6½
2½	1	1	9

Brush Flats, same.

Hooks.

1¼	1	5
1½	1	6
1¾	1	7
2	1	8
2¼	1	9
2½	1	10
2¾	1	11
3	2	0
3½	2	2
4	2	4
5	2	8
6	3	0
7	3	3½
8	3	7
9	3	10½
10	4	1½
12	4	8
14	5	3
18	6	3
20	6	9

Round Bills, 2d. per m more.
Fine Tucker, 1s. m more than Tiling Hooks

B. B. Horse.

4	3	0
5	3	2
6	3	5
7	3	8
8	4	0
9	4	4
10	4	8

YIELD.

2½ & 3oz.	30lb
5	32½
6	33
7	35
8 & 9	36
10	36½
11	37
12 & 13	39
14	40½
15	41½
16oz. to 1¼lb	42
1½	43
2 & 2¼	44
2½ & 2¾	45
3 to 4½	46
5 & 6	48
7	49
8	50
9 & 10	51
12 & 13	52
15	52½
16 to 19	53
20	53½
Larger,	54

Mid-century list of James Green of the Strand

The list price, drawn up and amended from time to time at the meetings of nailmasters, is often taken to have started in 1838 but the Sweating Commission Report made it clear that prices of nails were regulated by masters long before that date. In any case the list price was no more than nominal since it was frequently undercut by foggers and smaller masters.

In a list of 1842, to take one example, there are 44 classes of nails and in one class 27 different types and sizes. The list illustrated is from James Green of the Strand and is not much simpler. Looking at Flemish tacks—one of the small nails Bromsgrove was best known for—we have 'best' and 'fine' listed; but generally there were 'common', 'fine', and 'extra fine' varieties of most nails. Fine nails had a finer and longer tang and were more difficult to make than the common variety; while the extra fine were more difficult still. Consequently, their prices varied accordingly. The 8, 14 and 16oz types refer to the weight per 1000 nails but the price here refers to the cost per 1000 to the customer (not to the nailer).

The most common nails made by women and children were hob nails for boots and shoes. There are 73 different types and/or sizes in Lewis's catalogue and these were approximately 4½d per 1000 to make. But to add to the confusion the nailer paid by the *tale*, or 1000, actually handed over 1200 nails.

> It is necessary to remark that, by a pleasant little custom of the trade, a thousand nails, as between man and master, are twelve hundred nails, but only eight hundred (especially in the matter of hob nails) as between master and customer. Result, four hundred nails gratis in the warehouse. Thus 20,000 Flemish tacks means 24,000.[6]

Making a maximum of 20,000 (24,000) tacks a week, Sherard continues, a man

> would consequently produce 20 x 6½d = 10s 10d . . . deduct 6d for stalling and 9d for breeze . . . less 6d for wear and tear of his tools, leaving 9s 1d. This means that he has to make 220 tacks for 1d.[7]

After 1838 bates were regularly applied to wages in the nail trade. 'Bate' became the most feared word in the nailer's vocabulary. A bate of 10% meant £1 became 18/–, and if that position was not restored then a further bate

ate even more deeply into the original £1. A small crumb of comfort for the good nailer was the few extra nails he could make from skilful use of the 4/5 inches at the end of each of the three pieces into which the 5-foot rod was cut.

Until 1838 wages, though poor, were not quite desperate. There are accounts of good nailers earning 16/- a week on the better paid work—no hours mentioned, though. But generally speaking no more that 20,000 (24,000, of course) could be made by a nailer in a week of 80/90 hours; and if these nails were hobs or tacks, paid for at 4½d per 1000 as they were in some years, then a week's wages could be as little as 7/6d. For the nailer who owned or rented his nailshop there could be some extra income of 6d or 8d a week for each nailblock rented out to a staller as well as a contribution towards the cost of breeze.

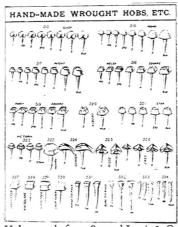

Hobs on sale from Samuel Lewis & Co Ltd of Withymoor, Dudley (about 1870)

Just before the 1914-18 War Jack Kings, my grandfather and an expert in making pig rings and clinkers, earned 21/- in one particular week. The word went round Bromsgrove as effectively as if Blind Joe (the town crier) had announced it himself: 'Jack Kings has earned a golden sovereign!'

The next person to handle that golden sovereign was Jimmy McDermott, landlord of the Red Lion, and my grandad celebrated in the time-honoured tradition.

Six

Nails in the coffin: a century of despair

Lads unite and better your conditions
When eggs are scarce, eggs are dear
When men are scarce, men are dear

So argued the miners of Durham soon after it became legitimate to combine in a union. It was not so easy for nailers. They were far from scarce, more like two a penny.

The story of the nail trade in the nineteenth century is one of increasing strife as nailers faced more and more cuts to their low wages; as foggers continued to pay in truck; as the nail-making machines took on more and more production; and as attempts were made to rescue once and for all nailers' children from the worst kind of inheritance.

With one exception the battles were lost. The children did eventually escape bellows and block after the campaigns of individual philanthropists finally convinced the government that it was time for all children to go to school. But by the end of the century wages were as abysmal as ever, nailers striking normally not for an increase but against a decrease. The fogger continued his illegal activities largely unchecked because he was dealing with a group of workers too poor and too scared to report him; not until the later decades of the century did the authorities show any real will to deal with the truck system which nailers found every bit as offensive as low wages. And machine nails rolled out of the factories in increasing numbers and varieties, gaining an ever larger slice of the home market. Alarm in the hand-wrought trade was evident as early as 1817 when a petition to the House of Commons expressed the conviction of the nailers of St. Ninian's and Falkirk that machines would be 'the ruin of the trade'. In 1907 the total value of nails produced in Great Britain was £534,000 of which only £51,000 were hand-wrought.[1] (On a slightly more cheerful note the brush nail, one of Bromsgrove's specialities, was one of the last to succumb to machine manufacture and continued to be made in this century).

The numerous strikes produced hardly any gains and the nailers remained in a weak position, devoid of any bargaining power. The trouble was there were far too many of them. Unlike many other crafts they had never controlled entry to their trade; anyone could set up—and did: wives and children, unemployed colliers and ironworkers, those with other jobs wanting to earn a little extra of an evening or weekend. As the century wore on too many were chasing too little work. Ironically, the very women and children who were drawn into nailing to help supplement the ever shrinking rewards swelled the ranks to the point of gross over-crowding. Between 1801 and 1851 the population of Bromsgrove nearly doubled from 5,898 to 10,310. The rise in the number of nailers was greater still, over 3,000 in 1851 compared to about 1,000 at the beginning of the century; and half of these were women, the really big increase in their numbers occuring in the 1840s when the bates began to be felt.

The very nature of the cottage nailing industry also made progress difficult. Its workers were scattered throughout towns and villages, by tradition badly paid and dealing only individually with masters and foggers. Not suprizingly an independent approach to his work remained the dominating characteristic of the nailer and it proved more or less impossible to persuade him that advances could be made only by concerted action.

As late as 1884, when many workers had been successfully organized into trade unions and societies for some years, Levett Nokes pleaded with nailers to get together in a way they had utterly failed to do in the past:

> Nailers have at all times been divided and selfish, and so they fall . . . if nailers were organized they would not be in the disgraceful and degraded position they are now in.[2]

When Joseph Arch visited Bromsgrove in 1875, Nokes recalled, he encouraged them to join the union which had then existed for some three years 'but after Mr Arch had pressed them they said, "No, we have managed our own affairs so long, and we will manage them still." Four years later the union folded.

In fairness to the nailers the problems inherent in their situation—as in all domestic industry—worked against organization; and it would have been difficult to pay the weekly 1d or 2d sub to fund attempts to secure better wages and conditions. But Nokes was not the only one to comment on the disinclination to unite: apart from a few localized and brief experiments in solidarity the hand-wrought nail trade remained unorganized to the end.

The tiswas (see p 91)

All this made life easy for the fogger (and the little masters who took their cue). Threatened by the machine, it was inevitable that cuts would be made:

> ... fourteen out of every fifteen reductions in our district originate from them, purely from those foggers.[3]

The nailmasters themselves were no better organized. The few big firms with a reputation for fair dealing were full of good intentions; but in practice they invariably followed the lead of the foggers and small masters, albeit after a short delay. Time and time again they lacked the strength and determination to force the mavericks to toe the line and pay the agreed prices. The Nailmasters Association was dissolved in 1879 following the admission that not enough masters were prepared to adhere to list prices.

As machinery was developed to make a greater range of nails faster and more cheaply than ever before the fogger was able to initiate a series of cuts in wages, sitting as he did between a labour force without clout and a group of masters without leadership.

Local nailers appear to have gone on strike as early as 1828. It's difficult to say more than that because although Palmer's Bromsgrove Almanack and Directory—first published in 1860—regularly records the anniversary of the 'great strike of Bromsgrove nailmakers' contemporary sources have, so far at least, shed no further light on the event (and Henry Ince, nailer, lay preacher and campaigner, makes no reference to the strike when looking back over his experience in the industry[4]). But a strike at that time would have been a distinct possibiltity as there is evidence of widespread unrest in both Bromsgrove and the Black Country.

From the records of William Robeson,[5] a Bromsgrove solicitor, some of whose business as magistrates' clerk was conducted on the order of the magistrates, we learn that a group of rioters from Redditch had been causing trouble, had been apprehended on the road to Droitwich and brought back to Bromsgrove where the following day, 7 December 1831, they were hauled before the bench:

> Attended at the Crown Inn, Bromsgrove, taking the examination of a man named Griffin against five persons from Redditch named Lilley, Paddock, Allcock, Andrews and Harman for abetting and advising Griffin to assist them in breaking the machines at Redditch.

For his services on this occasion Robeson claimed 18/6 plus 16/6 expenses, the former including 1/- fee for recording evidence against an unfortunate young man called Bourne, 'forward in the mob' and audacious enough to have shouted 'go it!' when the constables were dispersing the crowd. The high expenses included 13/6 for 'chaise hire' to Droitwich and back ('being very unwell' he chose this method of travel rather than the horse).

Three days after Christmas

> It having been hinted to Lord Plymouth and Lord Aston that a mob were quietly assembling at Bromsgrove in consequence of Mr Juggins reducing the price of nails

Robeson attended Hewell to advise Lord Plymouth and then on the following day acted as the intermediary at a day-long meeting at the Crown Inn between some of the town's 'principal Inhabitants' on the one hand and the nailmasters on the other. Plymouth and Aston were informed of the temporary compromise reached but clearly fearing trouble Robeson then arranged for the lordly magistrates to descend upon the town on the next day to swear in a number of special constables whom Robeson had lined up the previous evening.

Trouble certainly began to brew in the late 1830s however when the nailmasters, at a quarterly meeting, decided that owing to the depressed state of the trade and competition from the machine nail it was necessary to reduce wages.[6] A further bate (abatement of wages) took place the following year, in 1838, the masters this time expressing reluctance that in self-defence they were having to follow those who had already 'clandestinely' reduced wages. There is no record of any organized protest against either reductions but it is clear that the masters were divided, that the foggers and the little masters were already calling the tune. And it is almost certain that these and further bates were responsible for the large protest meeting held in 1841 when at least 15,000 nailers, including a large contingent who had walked from Bromsgrove, gathered in Dudley. Fearing serious consequences because the nailers were turning up at the collieries in Dudley in an effort to persuade the miners to join in, the Dudley magistrates called in the militia. The Troop of the 6th Dragoon immediately marched from their Birmingham barracks and remained in Dudley for two-and-a-half weeks.

Though the demonstration was kept under control[7] there must have been some bloodshed as the nailers sprinkled the ground between themselves and the dragoons with a weapon known as a *tiswas* ('tis as it was'), two pieces of nail iron bent together in the form of a tetrahedron, each of the four arms some 3 inches in length and ground to a point. The dictionary definition of 'tiswas' suggests a commotion, a state of excitement. A couple of thousand years earlier the Romans certainly caused that with their use of a similarly simple but vicious device known as the 'caltrop'.

In 1842 there was a very serious strike. On 19 April the masters met and announced a further reduction in wages, this time a 20% bate to take effect the following week. About 15,000 nailers marched on Dudley, captured some of the nailmasters en route and attempted to seize the Dudley masters. The militia was called out from Birmingham, the Riot Act was read and the crowd dispersed. In Bromsgrove Henry Ince took part in his first strike:

> The masters at that time paid 14s. to the £ (*ie* compared with the standard set in the 1838 list price). We nailers were very bad off, working for so little. A strike was called, and in about three or four weeks the masters consented to give us what is called 16s. to the £.[8]

Still, in other words, 20% down on the 1838 agreed prices.

In 1843 concern about the state of the nail trade in Bromsgrove reached the Times:[9]

> Last night the western neighbourhood of Birmingham was considerably excited and alarmed by rumours and disturbances amongst the turn-out nailers of Bromsgrove . . . About 7 o'clock a detachment of the 1st Royal Dragoons, under Captain Peel (the nephew of the Premier), left Birmingham at a head gallop, and arrived in Bromsgrove about half-past 8.

The reporter goes on to describe the reason for the strike—a further bate—the men's petition to the magistrates to induce them to act as arbitrators in the dispute, and the subsequent meeting in the Town Hall where the state of the trade was discussed, in particular fogging and trucking 'extensively carried on in the parish'.

Whoever the reporter was he clearly had sympathy for the nailers whose poor state he ends by describing but whose responsible approach he underlines. Despite the number of strangers in the town from Cradley and other areas 'no acts of violence have been committed, nor need any be apprehended'.

Between 1838 and 1863 there were five general strikes in the nail trade and a number of partial ones.[10] Henry Ince confirms this frequency, recalling 'no less than seven or eight strikes' in Bromsgrove between 1842 and 1869, the pattern always the same:

> So it went on, first a bate, then a strike . . . all to gain back a reduction from the list.[11]

Meanwhile there was little leniency for the nailer who strayed slightly. The town's brand new newspaper, the Bromsgrove and Droitwich Weekly Mesenger, reported that on 29 May 1860 at the Petty Sessions George Kings[12] of Messrs Dipple and Kings, nailmasters, charged three men—John Rogers, Henry Connard and David Albut—with neglecting to 'work in iron had out'. The first two nailers were sentenced to one month's hard labour, the third given a further fortnight to turn the said iron into nails. In July of that same year a twenty-year-old nailer, Benjamin Tilt, was charged with stealing a pair of trousers belonging to James Regan and selling them for 4/-. He was sentenced to four years penal servitude.

1862 brought rumours, then news, of 'up country' discontent, with meetings at Old Hill, Halesowen, Lye and Rowley Regis to protest against a 20% bate on certain nails. The Bromsgrove masters did not bate but the nailers were obviously on edge and the year was not without incident.

An open-air meeting in the Cattle Market to discuss wages and the truck system was chaired by Henry Ince. Ince, born into a nailing family in Bournheath in 1801, seems to have chaired many such meetings during his working life until his retirement after the 1869 strike. He also chaired the succession of committees, formed probably on an ad hoc basis, and often known as the Working Nailers Committee, which put the nailers' case to the masters on the numerous times it was necessary to do so and which operated in the absence of a union. Meetings of nailers were usually held in the Cattle Market, Crown Close or the Corn Exchange—depending on the nature of the problem under discussion—and were generally convened by a 'bellman' who travelled round the districts acquainting nailers with the latest news. Ince, an ardent Primitive Methodist and travelling preacher in the Birmingham Circuit, was always an advocate of conciliation and compromise, supporting a strike only as a last resort. With Henry in the chair all meetings began and ended with a hymn and prayer.

In the spring of 1862 the nailers of Bromsgrove were still in no mood to be organized. In the Cattle Market on St. Patrick's Day a speaker suggested they should unionize with subscriptions of 1d a week for men and ½d for women. It was turned down. But they were becoming more open in their criticism of truck, over 200 meeting in Worcester Street towards the end of June to discuss the evils of the system. The suggestion was made that nailers should combine to prosecute the trucksters and £1 was offered to add to the £5 already promised by Rev Dr Collis of Bromsgrove School 'upon the first conviction before the magistrates of a truckster'.[13] Nearly half of those attending then marched four abreast to the workhouse up the Birmingham Road to acquaint the guardians with their feelings.

A month later the Town Hall and its approaches were crowded with nailers eager to hear how the magistrates would deal with Mrs Louisa Wells of Sidemoor and Mr Samuel Norbury of Little Catshill, both describing themselves as nail manufacturers, both accused of having paid wages in truck.

The charge against Mrs Wells was that 'by the agency of her servant Solomon Crane' she entered into 'an illegal contract with Richard Taylor that the wages between him and Mrs Wells be expended by him in the purchase of grocery and other goods in her shop at Sidemoor'.[14] The court however was so crowded and the exictement so high that the magistrates felt the need to consult and announced judgment would be reserved for a further fortnight. Curiously, the local newspaper makes no further reference to the case. (And there, with great regret, we have to leave Mrs Wells since determined efforts—both here and in Worcester to establish the whereabouts of the nineteenth-century petty sessional records for Bromsgrove have failed.)

Samuel Norbury obviously lacked Mrs Wells' charisma. His case went ahead and he was found guilty of paying Thomas Lloyd of Sidemoor in provisions—flour, sugar, cheese and treacle—and 1/6d in money instead of the 8/10d he should have received for the nails he had made. Norbury was fined £5 plus costs.[15] The decision was greeted with tremendous enthusiasm.

The following week's newspaper printed two interestingly contrasting letters: one from the Rev Dr Collis who had at last been able to hand over his £5 and who wrote to applaud the decision of the magistrates; a second letter from a fervent supporter of the truck system, the well-known local solicitor Edward Housman, father of the poet and classical scholar, whose statue today occupies such a prominent part in the town.[16]

Delivering the nails (From 'The White Slaves of England', *Pearson's Magazine*)

The successful prosecution of Samuel Norbury showed that if only nailers would report instances of trucking the grip of the foggers could be broken.

They were slow to come forward however and truck continued for a number of years. But a few nailers did summon the courage to report on their masters and the activities of the local bench in 1863—a busy year—demonstrate the growing will to 'nail' the trucksters. In July, for example, John Hemming informed against John Skidmore, nail manufacturer of Sidemoor, the latter being found guilty of paying in truck instead of 'coin of the realm'. He was fined £10 and costs of 10/6d and warned that the fine for a second offence would be £20, for a third £100.[17] This was sterling stuff on the part of the local bench. A week later Samuel Norbury was in trouble again, this time informed against by nailer David Sandford. Norbury was fined £10 (double his previous fine of a year before) with14/6d costs and, very significantly, the informant awarded £5. Sandford was not the nailer Norbury had paid in truck but a representative of the local nailers' committee who were clearly taking to heart the suggestion that they should combine to prosecute the trucksters.

At the same court Alfred Burford informed against James Heague, nail fogger of Worcester Street, the latter fined £7 and 10/6d costs with £2 of the fine going to the informant. £2 was the equivalent of three good weeks' wages. It was massive encouragement and the trucksters should have been on the run. They simply became more cunning, as 'the little performance' described by William Laugher shows;[18] and the fear of getting no iron remained a powerful incentive to keep quiet.

In August David Sandford was busy again, this time on behalf of nailer William Trumper. As a result Richard Hodgkiss, shopkeeper and nail fogger of Catshill, was fined £5 and 16/- costs for paying in truck, the magistrates reiterating their warning about stiffer penalties. Encouraged no doubt by these successes the Nailers' Anti-Truck Society was set up in the early autumn. The Report of the Truck Commission in 1871 suggests the new Society took out eight summonses against foggers, seven of whom were convicted; and it is interesting to note that donations towards its work came from several local clergymen, some of the bigger nailmasters and a number of 'respectable' shopkeepers.

As well as a series of truck prosecutions 1863 saw another strike. In May the nailmakers again announced a 10% reduction. Over 10,000 nailers went on strike, including those in the Bromsgrove area, Rowley Regis, Old Hill and Bartley Green; and large numbers of horse-nail makers also struck. The causes of the strike went deeper than the 10% bate, however, for this was a strike against the truck system; and had there been effective organization it would no doubt have been even more widespread. The nailers were out for eight weeks, threats of bellows-cutting suggesting, at the start at least, that it might prove a violent affair. Locally, nailers' leaders—Job Davies, Henry Ince, David Sandford and George Giles—all urged against violence. An editorial in the local newspaper worked out (perhaps overestimated) the loss to the town as '£1000 per week . . . the small shopkeeper, no longer able to give credit, will be ruined'.[19]

The local masters must also have been conscious of the effects the strike was having in the area for at the end of July 'in order to put a stop to the distress that exists' they offered to return to paying 20/- in the £, for two months at any rate, at which point if the up-country masters had not followed suit wages would have to be reduced accordingly. 1500 nailers gathered in the Cattle Market and voted on the recommendation of their leaders (one brave hand opposing) to go back to work. The gentry were thanked for their support, a unanimous vote against truck taken and the nalers' leaders given three hearty cheers.

Five years later the substantial nail manufacturing firm of Eliza Tinsley and Co announced a 20% bate. Other up-country masters did likewise. The result was an all-out strike in the Black Country. To 'clarify the situation' the nailers' leaders in Bromsgrove called a meeting which gave firm notice that any local attempt at a similar reduction would be met with by a general strike. It was better to starve at rest than at hard work, was the conviction of those gathered. A series of further meetings in the town centre, in Sidemoor, Bournheath, Catshill and Lickey End gained practical support for up-country brethren in the form of a weekly levy—4d for men, 2d for women—which the Bromsgrove nailmasters agreed to collect at source. A number of local nailmasters were non-conformists and though on occasions lacking courage and vision had genuine sympathy for the plight of the nailers. Financial and practical help from them was not uncommon; but particularly intriguing at this point was the fact that the Bromsgrove manager of Eliza Tinsley was levying nailers in order to support striking workers in the up-country branches of his firm.

On 2 January 1869 the annual dinner of the local Conservative party was held and was, it seems, 'good, abundant and well-served, the wines excellent and the dessert plentiful. The room was tastefully decorated with evergreens, flowers and the appropriate mottoes.' And amongst the toasts were the town and trade of Bromsgrove.[20] The leading trade in Bromsgrove needed much more than a salutory toast; before long its members were to be faced with starvation wages.

Towards the end of February an editorial in the local newspaper expressed concern at rumours of a further bate up-country,[21] following which nailmaster Edward Perkins of the Oakalls wrote to assure the public that the trade, contrary to the previous week's editorial, was in better shape than usual.[22] It was the editor's finger that was on the pulse. In the spring various groups of Black Country nailers went out on strike following a 10% bate. The Bromsgrove nailmasters took no decision for a while; then, near the end of May, announced a 10% reduction on the 1864 list prices, following, they explained, the reduction in Dudley and surrounding districts.

At the beginning of the strike the chairman of the magistrates, Mr Francis Watt, felt obliged to warn nailers in general—and nailer Byng of the Putcheon in particular—that any children sent out to beg would be treated as vagrants.[23] More constructively, the Local Board announced a public meeting on 7 June in the Town Hall to discuss ways off disbursing to those in distress a tidy sum of money in their possession. The money amounted to £329.2.9, £198.10.0 raised from a previous strike for purchasing soup for the poor (Why so much was still in their hands is not clear); and the rest, £130.12.9, from a Labour Fund by which money was raised for iron during bad times, nails were stored in the workhouse and then sold when trade improved. £130.12.9 was transferred to a 'relief fund' and a committee set up to administer it. The committee, consisting almost entirely of the acknowledged leaders of the working nailers, lost no time in distributing £70 worth of bread—4,000 4lb loaves.

There was clearly considerable sympathy for the striking nailers and at least one nailmaster, George Dipple, took it upon himself to distribute soup to the neediest. It is not entirely suprizing therefore that, when after ten weeks Bromsgrove masters agreed to return to the full 1864 list price and the men resumed work, a celebratory tea took place with masters and men sitting down together.

The relief committee had arranged for presentations to be made on the occasion: a walnut writing case for Mr Barratt, treasurer and Local Board member, and a whole new outfit for the man who had led them with dignity and common sense for so long but who was now retiring (in theory anyway. In practice he continued to be actively involved).

> ... Mr Henry Ince received the following: frock coat, waistcoat and trousers in superfine black cloth by Mr Hall of the Market Place, silk hat, pocket handkerchief, pair of boots, spectacles and case, silk stockings, garters and a

walking stick.[24]

Now the man they so so respected would be able to speak and meet with anyone on equal terms; and for his finale he retired to a side room, donned his new clothes, reappeared 'and brought the house down'.

Thus the year that had seen the introduction of the 'starvation list' and a two-and-a-half months' strike ended amicably and in some style.

Toward the end of August 1875 a very large number of nailers gathered on the present Recreation Ground in Bromsgrove, called together by leaders of the Bromsgrove Nail Forgers Protection Association to listen to a number of speakers, principally Joseph Arch, the nationally known campaigner and General Secretary of the Agricultural Workers Union, and Richard Juggins, the youthful Secretary of the Nut and Bolt Makers Association, a man who was to make such an impact on Bromsgrove nailers 16 years later. It was by all accounts a good natured affair and local leaders were able to announce that membership stood at 600 and funds at £900.[25]

The Association had been set up at the beginning of 1872 and was thus well into its fourth year. (An attempt to set up a union in 1868 had very quickly died the death.) Arch's plea for more members may have fallen on deaf ears but the Association carried on. Those were comparatively good times—a brief boom in the early seventies—and Bromsgrove nailmasters were paying 10% above other nailing districts. Nailers' leaders must have been conscious of this as they advised caution and patience following a move to seek higher wages. A small committee of nailers and masters produced a new list of prices averaging 7½%, a figure that was accepted in the autumn by the nailers despite some dissatisfaction.

It was yet another strike in 1877 however that broke the back of the infant Association. Bromsgrove nailmasters had demonstrated they were prepared to act independently of up-country masters. Now one of them decided to show he could act independently of his fellow town masters. At the beginning of the year Daniel Roper of the High Street, nail manufacturer, landlord of the King's Head and a few years later a member of the Town District Board, declared a 10% bate as orders began to grow short. The other nailmasters quickly made their position clear: unless the Bromsgrove Nail Forgers Protection Association could persuade Roper to reinstate list prices they too would reduce wages by 10%. After a couple of meetings the Association came up with a reasonable compromise: it would look after union members working for Roper if the masters would find work for Roper's non-union members. The masters declined the offer and a particularly fierce and bitter strike began, all but a handful of nailers stopping work.

The Local Board launched a public appeal and by the beginning of April had distributed £95 in the form of bread. The Association began by paying its full members (men) 10/- a week, its half-members (women) 5/-; and strikers held fast against the suggestion that nailers working for those masters now prepared to pay the list price should be allowed to return.

But Association funds were running out. Strike pay was reduced to 4/- for men and 2/- for women and later, in June, to less than half that. At the end of May it was agreed that those working for the several masters prepared to pay the list price should be allowed to start work again, paying a levy of 3/- a week to help support the rest. In June several more masters agreed to pay the list price but the few who insisted on a 10% bate finally won the day and towards the end of the month the rest of the nailers drifted back after twenty weeks on strike. Two years later Bromsgrove Nail Forgers Protection Association folded. It had no funds and insufficient support.

Throughout the 1870s and '80s the trade continued 'in a deplorable condition' with 'much privation and sickness'.[26] In 1887 an article in the Birmingham Daily Post pointed out that in the previous dozen years nailers' wages had fallen from between 55% and 65%.[27] Not suprizingly, nailers in a number of districts pushed for increases in wages and failing to achieve anything came out on strike. Almost all Bromsgrove nailmasters had agreed in principle to pay an extra 10% but in practice failed to do so, following this time the line of their up-country brethren. Even Mr B H Sanders, Clerk to the Local Board, made a bold attempt on the nailers' behalf, writing on 1 October to the up-country masters to urge them to increase wages as the Bromsgrove masters had agreed, in theory, to do. The reply was negative and later that month nailers once more returned to work with nothing to show for their hardship.

One aspect of the strike seems to have gone well, though. This was the organizing of a 'soup and bread fund' which dispensed provisions from the brewery in St John Street. On 24 October, for example, 880 children and 250 adults had been served bread and soup; on 28 October 1100 children and 150 adults.[28]

1887 was also the year a certain gentleman advertized for a wife. Among the 800 replies was one from a Bromsgrove lady who, in stressing her assets, claimed her father had 'died and left her 4 cows and £120'.[29] How many a single nailmaker must have longed for such a 'virtuous' wife.

Seven   A striking finale

> I have enquired into the sweating* system in the principal
> centres of England and I have concluded that among the
> nailmakers the povery is very often much greater than even
> among the sweated tailors in great towns.

Thus concluded the sanitary commissioner for The Lancet in his evidence
to the Select Committee on Sweating. The Committee's report appeared
in 1888 along with another report prepared by the Labour Correspondent
of the Board of Trade solely on the conditions of the nailmakers and
chainmakers of South Staffordshire and North Worcestershire. The findings
of both reports should have frightened the life out of the House of
Commons. The dismal state of nailmakers was graphically described, the
continuing employment of women and children castigated.

But commissions had come and gone for nearly half a century by then
with nothing of practical use done for the makers of hand-wrought nails.
Despite the Sweating Commission's claim that

> for at least 150 years the conditions of the nailers had been
> wretched in the extreme

the 1888 reports were filed away, as usual. But if the Government was not
prepared to attempt any practical reform others were. A great deal of disquiet
was expressed in the liberal press, particularly The Manchester Sunday
Chronicle; and the Fabian Society campaigned energetically for a better
deal for workers, especially those in the nail and chain trades.

Bitterness in the chain industry was brought to a head in 1890 by a trade
union leader of great charisma, Richard Juggins. Twenty years earlier

---

* The accepted shorthand for a combination of low wages, long hours and unhealthy working
conditions.

Juggins, son of a miner killed in a pit accident, had founded the Nut and Bolt Makers Association. As its part-time secretary he had been regarded by his employer as an agitator and duly dismissed. He then became the full-time secretary of the Midland Counties Trades Federation.

Like Bromsgrove's Henry Ince, Juggins was a lay preacher and man of great integrity. He also had considerable vision, in 1890 harnessing on behalf of women chainmakers the support of The Manchester Sunday Chronicle, the Fabian Society, Liberal MPs and many sympathetic organisations. Striking for 100% rise seemed ridiculous.* But a 50% rise for making small chains was achieved which gave all chainmakers some pride and some hope; and the organisation of that campaign was to be used with similar success eighteen months later.

At the end of March 1891 a meeting of nailmakers in the Town Hall, Bromsgrove, discussed a proposed Bill to restrict female labour along with the 'wages question'. What was felt of much more importance was the reward for their labour, whether it was male or female. Consequently it was moved that no Bill would be satisfactory unless it contained this clause:

> That all employers of labour shall publish in their warehouse a list of prices. That it would be penal on their part to violate that list without 14 days' notice, and that they should supply their workmen with a note stating the quantity of nails weighed and the sum paid.[1]

Mr J H Green, it was pointed out, was not paying the list price and it was unanimously agreed that the following day the nailmakers should march in a body to his warehouse and get his men to withdraw their labour. At this stage it was believed that another nailmaster, another Mr Green, of the Strand would take on twenty of J H Green's men and the Joint Stock Warehouse a further twenty.

The Joint Stock Company (The Bromsgrove Nailers' Cooperative Society) was probably the most successful bit of local nailing cooperation in the history of the trade. Founded during the strike of 1887 and properly registered two years later under an Act of Parliament it had an office and warehouse from which it distributed iron and to which the nailers returned their finished nails to be disposed of by the Society on the open market. It had a president, secretary and managing committee, all volunteers; and members paid 1/- entrance fee and contribution of 3d per week. At the

---

* As daft as choosing a Bromsgrove Rovers team from the Thursday OAP queue.

end of 1889 it had 179 members, 20 working full-time for the Society; and its aim was to reach a stage when all members could work direct for it.[2] The Society always paid its employees top prices and often as much as 30% more than was paid by nailmasters. It existed for some twenty years, succumbing largely due to the petering out of the industry itself.

An old Bromsgrove nailer (From 'The White Slaves of England', *Pearson's Magazine*)

The last know reference to the Society's activities comes from the Bromsgrove and Droitwich Weekly Messenger on 6 February 1909 when members of the Bromsgrove Nailforgers Ltd (it had changed its name at least a decade earlier) gathered in the schoolroom of Ebenezer Methodist Church in Sidemoor for another AGM. The cooperative was in good shape: its long-standing secretary, Mr James Powell, was able to report that funds were good; that £9 was now being paid on the death of a member or his wife; and that £2.2.0 would be donated to the Cottage Hospital.

In a suitable skirmish for the first day of April 1891 more than one hundred nailers gathered in Sidemoor to march to the offending J H Green's warehouse. There was still no union in Bromsgrove. Leaders, yes: they always emerged; and a young cooperative society was able to help to some extent. But there hadn't been a union for twelve years. Mr Green was not there. Nor was he at home in New Road (wise man!). But other masters agreed to take on Green's men at the list price and by the time the men reached the Town Hall they were acquainted with the news that J H was now prepared to pay the proper rate. Things appeared to settle down.

By the end of October Black Country nailers—first in Halesowen, then Old Hill, Blackheath and Rowley—all went out on strike, unable to continue the struggle on miserable wages. But Bromsgrove nailers bided their time despite the encouragement of James Powell of the Nailers' Cooperative Society to join in and support their brothers and sisters.

A week later however it was very different.* Richard Juggins addressed the nailers in the Cattle Market arguing that a strike for a 10% increase was a puny affair, the equivalent of only 2d a day for most of them. The Manchester Sunday Chronicle, so supportive of the chainmakers during their successful strike, had announced they would give £100 to the funds if nailmakers joined a union and struck not for a 10% but a 50% increase. (Though no written resolution has been unearthed, the decision to strike must have been taken at this meeting.) A few days later the nailers were informed that the Chronicle's pledge had been renewed as well as a further offer made to raise a public subscription on their behalf—and the local paper similarly urged them to combine together in a union as had the dockers of London and the chainmakers of Dudley.

Before the month of November was out they did precisely that—on a unanimous vote in the presence of the editor of The Manchester Sunday Chronicle, Mr T Harris, and Richard Juggins, the town's most dynamic and frequent visitor. Harris reported that working men up North had been astounded by the particulars of the nailers' conditions, at first disbelieving and then, when shown the truth, concluding that their nailing brethren must be 'a complete set of fools' to stand for it! Mr Harris was also able to announce that subscriptions were arriving from all over the country and £50 had been received from a gentleman in the South of France.

The Chronicle's offer was dependent upon the strike being an all-out and properly organized one; and the demand being for a 50% all-round increase. Despite initial enthusiasm the nailers of Halesowen and Old Hill returned to work for a 10% increase after only a few days. But Bromsgrove had the bit between its teeth. Its nailers, now organized into the Bromsgrove Amalgamated Union of Wrought Nail Makers, under the secretaryship of Elijah Albutt, turned down a similar offer. (Curiously, though, since the Union was not registered until 23 December 1892—under the name of Mr W Maskell of Church Lane, Sidemoor—it remained unofficial until

---

* Much of the following account of the 1891/2 strike is based on the weekly reports of the Bromsgrove and Droitwich Weekly Messenger from 7 November 1891 to 29 February 1892; and The Manchester Sunday Chronicle from 25 October to 22 November 1891.

long after this great strike finished.)

By now nailers were getting help and advice from all corners. In December campaigning visitors included Mr de Mattos, an executive member of the Fabian Society, who spoke to the nailers about the strikes he had experienced; and a few days before Christmas there was a promise of a free Christmas Day tea for 400 and a further £100 for union funds. Outside support was tremendous: over £400 was collected from the public and from other unions to enable the strikers to stay out.[3] And the nailers of Bromsgrove remained solidly behind their new union, continuing to reject anything less than a 50% rise in wages. The day before Christmas Eve Richard Juggins and the Misses Abrams and Conway of the Fabian Society were met by a procession at the station in Aston Fields and escorted into the town where they spoke to a packed meeting in the Town Hall.

Christmas came and went while the main features of the strike continued unaltered: distinguished visitors arrived to give words of encouragement (on 18 January, for instance, it was Rev John Trevor of the Labour Church in Manchester) and to pass on donations; nailers turned out in great throngs for the almost bewildering numbers of meetings in the town's larger buildings and open spaces; and resolutions in favour of a 50% rise continued to be unanimous.

On 16 January a church parade comprised nailers from the Lickey, Lickey End, Staple Hill, Sidemoor, Catshill and Bournheath. The procession formed in fours with 800 men and women headed by the Aston Fields Drum and Fife Band. At the church the Vicar, Rev Vine Hall, preached on 'God is Love' (John 4 v16), acknowledging that some present might not agree that the Ruler of the Universe was kind and merciful. The procession reformed outside the church and the parade was led by the Cradley Heath Chainmakers' Brass and Reed Band. An open-air meeting was held under the Hallelujah Lamp at the bottom of the town.

The following week a very large meeting must have listened with great attention as Richard Juggins announced the latest donations to the Bromsgrove nailers' cause:

> *Lincolnshire—£5-13-8*
> *The Society of Lacemakers, Nottingham—£10*
> *Union of Dock Labourers, Birkenhead—£3-10-0*
> *Birmingham Job Printing Guild—15/-*
> *Mr Corbett's Ginger Beer Works—5/- for every week of the strike*

Mr Tangye—15 guineas
An Oldham butcher—2 loads of salted heads of pigs and other
meats plus £1
The Amalgamated Society of Engineers—a levy of 2d per
member
A telegram was received from Manchester saying that another
£100 was on its way

The meeting closed (as usual)with the Doxology.

Less than a week later the inhabitants of Bromsgrove were again reminded (as if they could have forgotten) that these were special times. This time the event was organized by Ike Ward of the General Railway Workers Union, beginning with the roasting of a 9cwt ox in the yard of the Coach and Horses. This was followed by a procession of Bromsgrove nailers and supporters, some 2,000, who paraded through the town, the women addressed at the Corn Exchange by Miss Conway (on a return visit), the men at the Recreation Ground by Richard Juggins who read out a message from Mr T Harris pledging £200 a week to the strikers on behalf of the Chronicle. Other contributions announced were more humble but gratefully received, no doubt: 700 penny cakes from Mr G Curtis and a supply of carrots from Mr Burton.

At the end of January the masters upped their offer to 20% but after some discussion this was overwhelmingly (though not unanimously) rejected. An incident shortly after must have helped release some of the tension. One of the magistrates, Mr Thomas White, had made derogatory remarks in public at the police court about the nailers and their strike. It did not go down well. A procession was organized through Catshill with an effigy of the unloved JP at its head. The marchers must have been encouraged to hear that another magistrate, Mr John Amphlett, had taken exception to the remarks and had slapped Mr White's face. Proceeding to the Recrettion Ground in the town they burnt the effigy to the singing of 'Poor Old Jeff, he's gone to rest'.

The most unusual support for the strike came the following month from a circus. On Wednesday 17th February 1892 Wombwell and Bailey's International Circus gave a performance to a packed audience on behalf of the Bromsgrove nailers. The show was preceded by a gigantic torchlight procession through Birmingham—elephants, cmaels, clowns, trapeze artists, military bands—and Mr Wombwell introduced Richard Juggins, John Smith, of the chainmakers' union, and Ike Ward, the latter making a speech on behalf of the strikers. It was a dazzlingly different occasion though less than outstanding in terms of money collected: from the centre of Birmingham £20, from the fleshpots of Edgbaston 4/6d.

The following day representatives of the nailers met the Bromsgrove masters—and some of the principal up-country masters—at the Midland Hotel, Birmingham. Juggins gave the employers a fortnight to make a more substantial offer, then sped back to Bromsgrove to advise the nailers to refuse to take any iron from the masters but instead work for the Co-operative which would leave them better off.

On the last day of February it was unanimously agreed that, as terms rung from the masters would lead to nailers being better off by an average of 30-35%, there should be an immediate return to work. The last long strike was over. It had been conducted with great common sense and determination; and there was not the bitterness of some earlier strikes. The widespread support—from friends, trade unionists, the public, the press—meant that a strike fund could pay 4/6d a week to men, 2/3d a week to women, a very substantial proportion of what they would have received from full-time work. But the most crucial factor in the strike's success was undoubtedly the charisma and ability of Richard Juggins. He it was who provided the motivation, inspiration and organizing flair to achieve the rise they did.

Three months later, towards the end of May 1892, 112 people sat down to a dinner in the Coach and Horses, among them all those individuals connected with the strike, including the proprietor and editor of The Manchester Sunday Chronicle. A letter of apology was read from Austen Chamberlain MP. Afterwards, a procession headed by the Cradley Heath Chainmakers' Brass Band went through the High Street to the Recreation Ground where over 2,000 people were waiting. Presentations were made to the Chronicle's proprietor, Edward Hulton—a framed address; to his son and to his editor—gold scarf pins; and to Richard Juggins who was presented with a 'nice little pony and a handsome trap'. The harness had a silver inscription reading:

> Presented to R Juggins Esq., Darlaston, by the Bromsgrove
> nailmakers after the strike of 1891/2

Sadly, the 'peace with honour' agreement did not lead to a new and happier era in the history of the trade. Markets were disappearing too fast and in 1894 there was a new reduction on the 1892 list of 10%. Distressing too is the sour note which marked the end of the nailers' union in Bromsgrove. During the strike there had been some 1400 members, some of whom the union had kept in work by providing with iron and buying their nails. When the strike ended there was an estimated 12-15 tons of nails in stock worth between £500 and £600. The euphoria at the end of the strike was soon replaced by the old apathy and union membership rapidly declined; and a move to wind up the union in 1895 and share its assets between paid-up members led to great acrimony not only within the union but within the town itself, a number of leading citizens—Emma Rea, Albert Giles, Moses Nokes—writing to the newspaper to express their opposition or support. Perhaps it was just as well that Richard Juggins died in March 1895, ignorant of the undignified squabbling which marked the end of organized attempts to unionize the nail trade in Bromsgrove.*

The Bromsgrove nailshop, 1896 (From 'The White Slaves of England', *Pearson's Magazine*)

* Another major figure in the strike, the Chronicle's editor, had died a few months after the strike ended.

The 1914—18 War all but killed off the dying nail trade, for so long the area's staple industry. The fortunate survivors of those years of mayhem returned to blighty determined to leave nails well alone and enter newer, better paid jobs. As the old nailers died, so did the trade itself. But for the few years between the wars those left did comparatively well. The trade was no longer grossly overstocked and certain types of hand-wrought nails were in demand still—brush nails, for example, alpine clinkers, some of the hob nails. I can remember taking my grandfather's nails to Parry's warehouse in Church Road, Catshill, and coming back with £3, a wage not far short of the skilled toolmaker's at the time, a wage earlier nailmakers would have received with disbelief. On the other hand, he probably worked between 70 and 80 hours for it, nearly twice as long as the toolmaker.

But the same James Parry of Catshill obviously felt in 1920 that, with some capital and modernisation, the ailing industry could be re-established. He had been interviewed in his warehouse by a reporter from The Graphic and extracts of the encounter were reproduced in The Messenger of 6 March along with editorial comment. William Emus of Golden Cross Lane clearly thought both Parry and The Messenger had got carried away!

> *Sir: The nailmakers at Catshill have been aware for some months past that they and their industry were receiving more than ordinary attention from both enquiring visitors and photographers. Some of us had been discussing the reason for all this, until the issue of the "Messenger" last Saturday, when we were astonished at some of the statements . . . If the writer had spoken of the declension instead of the revival of the trade, he would have been nearer the mark . . . For example . . . I will take Barley Mow Lane. In this particular lane there were fifty-one nailshops, but at present only eight are occupied by nail makers; the others remain vacant, or are used for other purposes, and that leaves forty-three with a very remote chance of ever being used for their former purposes. This is typical of the industry at Catshill . . . The statment as to wages needs to be greatly qualified . . . After working at hand nailmaking for over 20 years, and being in the trade still, I consider the average wage of male operators, after working expenses are paid, is £3 a week, unless the worker sells his work.*

William Emus was Catshill's last nailmaker, along with Charlie Troth the subject of an article published in The New Statesman and Nation on

28 June 1952 when he was still making brush nails in his wash house 'still used for the purpose it had served since Queen Victoria was a slip of a girl'. Frank Weaver of Golden Cross Lane made brush nails until the end of the Second World War; and Walter Kings, also of Golden Cross Lane, was still active as nailmaker and master, that rare breed, a staunch non-conformist whose stature may be measured by the fact that when he stood for the Board of Guardians for North Bromsgrove he received 206 votes compared to his opponent's 13. Henry Fisher, the last nailmaker in Bournheath, finished at the outbreak of the Second World War; but evidence of the trade remains in the village despite the additions, conversions, improvements, expansions made to original cottages and workshops. In Sidemoor Mrs Rea of Providence Road seems to have been the last woman nailer, like Henry Fisher giving up on the eve of war. But Albert Crane of Broad Street and Charlie Troth of York Road, Sidemoor, carried on for a few more years. Charlie's favourite saying when reminiscing about the trade was 'Glory gone!'. Unfortunately, he would never allow conversations to be recorded nor filming of him at work. But his conclusion was always the same:

It was a clemmin' trade—when I die let it die with me.

Eight   Chapel, pub and pigeons

What did nailers do in their spare time? A catch question, perhaps. Yet, long though their hours were, there was usually something to life apart from nailmaking.

In the second half of the nineteenth century nailers were described in some quarters as an irreligious, drunken and immoral lot. Even if it were true it would hardly be surprizing: people who live cheek-by-jowl in such poverty and misery, year in year out, may well be forgiven for losing sight of their worth and their pride, for failing to rise to the finer things in life. But in any case the view is a sweeping one, bolstered by those with little knowledge of and interest in the closely packed community of nailers.

Certainly the Bromsgrove area produced its fair share of nailer-preachers and nailers played a leading part in a number of the nonconformist chapels that sprung up in and around the town. The Methodist lay preachers were the ones who made most headway amongst the nailers as the nineteenth century progressed. Unlike their Anglican brothers (and to a large extent Baptist and Congregational ministers who on the whole attracted the more 'respectable' working class), they were more often than not from the same background as the nailers, speaking the same language and with the same accent.

First and foremost there was Henry Ince, not only a respected leader among nailers, a champion of the poor and oppressed—called on occasions 'the nailmaker's Joseph Arch'—but also an ardent Methodist. He was born in 1801 into a Bournheath nailing family, joined the Primitive Methodists as a young man and soon began preaching locally. By his early thirties he was a recognized travelling preacher employed by the Birmingham Circuit (earning, incidentally, 9/- a week which was nearly as much as he would have been paid for many more hours of nailmaking). According to Rev Arthur Wilkes who heard him preach,[1] Ince possessed an iron constitution and wonderfully loud voice which could be heard a mile away!

In one particularly hot summer, 'when the wells were empty, the springs dry and the crops in danger of being scorched' Ince preached in Catshill on the subject of heaven—in local accent to local people:

> When we gettin' ta 'eaven, we shall ha' grass up to 'ur knees, and wate (wheat) forty threave to the yeacre and calico a fardin' a yard, an' we shall be yeable to see through a cast metal wall forty mile thick!

Hell was also a favourite subject:

> If yo' gettin' ta' 'ell, if yo' gettin' ta' 'ell, a boat looad o' prayers wunt fatch ya out agen!

Henry Ince

As well as his preaching engagements in the Coventry and Stratford areas Henry Ince spoke at many local venues, including Hephzibah, the Primitive Methodist chapel on the Birmingham Road, built in 1861 and still standing. A number of the chapel's original trustees were nailers. In all probability he preached in Sidemoor too where in about 1820 a group of Primitive Methodists (ie those who claimed a return to Wesley's first principles) was formed, probably as a result of nailers having heard the preaching of Thomas Brownsford, a Primitive Methodist on his way from Worcester to

Stourbridge.[2]

But Sidemoor produced its own crop of nonconformist preachers, most notably those of the Crane family who for so long led Ebenezer Methodist Church in Broad Street. Through the generosity of David Troth who gave the land and a man called Ellins (the wealthy nail manufacturer, perhaps?) who gave the materials, a small stone chapel was built in 1838. So poor was its largely nailing congregation however that within five years the chapel was on the verge of having to be sold when Jeremiah Grant, a member of the Wesleyan church on the Kidderminster Road, bought the chapel and at the age of 70 became its first minister.[3]

Most Primitive Methodists at that time were referred to in derogatory terms as 'Ranters' because of the spontaneous, fervent and loud participation in the services of both preacher and congregation, in stark contrast to the tone which prevailed in the established church. Whatever his approach, Grant built up the little congregation and when he died in 1856 James Crane, nailer's toolmaker, was unanimously called by the members to become leader.

James, it is said, was converted when he was twenty partly as a result of having witnessed a fight on The Common (Broad Street) in which a man was killed.[4] When James died in 1856, after 30 years of devoted service, his son William took over, leading the congregation for a further 30 years. The Cranes certainly loom large in Ebenezer's history; but so, even more, do nailers. The chapel's deeds are littered with the names of nailmakers and nail factors—Josiah Dyers, Solomon Crane, Charles Troth, Benjamin Nickless, Sam Bane, Richard Crawford. At every stage in its history, it seems, there were nailers willing to take on the responsibilities that the work of the chapel involved. In this century another two stalwart members of Ebenezer, Albert Crane and Charlie Troth, were among the very last nailers in the area.

In Catshill the nailing community was located in that part of the village which used to be called Little, occasionally Upper, Catshill (though just to confuse the issue it was the bigger of the two Catshills). Little Catshill was the radical, nonconformist side of the Spadesbourne as opposed to Big, or Lower, Catshill which was solidly Tory and contained the Anglican church, the vicarage and the school. The Primitive Methodists began preaching in the Little Catshill area in the 1820s, firstly in the open air, then in the following decade in a rented room in Barley Mow Road, until the first purpose-built chapel was erected in 1851 to house 200 (a great act of faith, since membership at the time was only 30 and the whole village numbered no more than 450!). Fifteen years later an even bigger chapel was built for this vigorous group of churchgoers and once again nailers not only filled many of the seats but undertook preaching and administrative duties on top of their week's work.

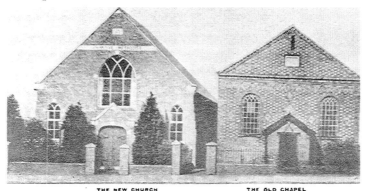

THE NEW CHURCH   THE OLD CHAPEL

Primitive Methodist Chapel, Catshill (From *Our Chapel*)

Thomas Wilkes, father of Rev Arthur Wilkes—author of *Our Chapel* written in 1931—preached in the area for twenty years and was a leading figure in the formation of the Nailers' Union; Joseph Gwynne taught in the Sunday School and took particular pride in keeping the chapel clean; Ambrose Waldron, a highly skilled nailer with a reputation for being able to turn his hand to anything, was a preacher and Sunday School teacher, became prosperous from a plot of land farmers had declared barren for a century and lived for a time in America; the Goode brothers, Henry and George, were both devoted servants of the church; and Enoch Rutter, one of the most interesting of the Primitive Methodist pioneers, was a railway worker until rheumatism forced him to retire, at which point he taught himself nailing—so efficiently that he was able to save up, buy a bit of land, build his own cottage, open a village shop and become a successful market gardener. And all this he combined with regular preaching duties.

But the Primitive Methodists did not quite have a monopoly among nailers. In 1828 a small Baptist community was established in Catshill, entirely as a result of the series of cottage meetings conducted by Moses Nokes, a member of the Baptist church in Bromsgrove who was convinced of the need to go and preach to the nailers rather than wait and hope they found their own way to church. The extent of nailers' influence on the growth of the chapel may be judged by the fact that when new trustees were appointed in 1875 no less than seven of the fifteen were nailers. And it is good to note that in this century at least one or two nailers—such as William Emus—bridged the denominational gap by preaching regularly to both Primitive Methodists and Baptists.

Nor were the nailmasters themselves all either heathen or Anglican (as might be supposed!). Nail factors Josiah Dyers and Amos Miles were closely associated with Ebenezer in its early years; Edward Perkins (chief warehouse in the High Street, private residence the Oakalls) was a great supporter of Windsor Street Congregational Chapel (now the United Reform Church); Henry Parry, nail manufacturer in Worcester Street and later—in the early years of this century—John Grove, nail factor in the Strand, were both associated with the work of New Road Baptist Church; and in Catshill Walter Kings, maker and manufacturer, of Brumfil's Row was an active lay preacher.

Despite the significant part played by the nailers in many local churches statements continued to be made about their lack of interest in anything religious. In his October 1868 report Inspector Fitton said:

> . . . Few attend any place of worship. Almost none go to church, some few attend the Ranters.[6]

Thirty years later, on the other hand, Robert Sherard begins his account of his study of Bromsgrove nailers by remarking that 'the Bromsgrove nailmaker is both God-fearing and simple' and ends by quoting a Sidemoor nailer:

> I have never had my wages here, but when I get to Heaven I shall get my reward and my oppressor will get his . . . I am living in the hopes of Heaven.[7]

Whether or not the average nailer attended chapel he usually made sure his children did, a fact reflected in the very high Sunday School rolls in the nineteenth and early twentieth century. Before the 1870 Education Act more and more nailers saw Sunday Schools as a way of starting their sons and daughters on the road to reading and writing and out of nailing altogether; and for children, clean from the weekly bath and donned in best clothes (if they had any), Sunday School must have represented a very different experience from the grind of the week, the once-a-year Sunday

School treat—with sports, prizes and sweets—the highlight of the year. A bible or other book would often have been the only reading matter in the cottage.

Sunday was a rest day for one and all, a break from the physical demands of the workshop, a 'cooked meal' day with meat on the menu. The men were sometimes accused of carrying on every Sunday from where they were presumed to have left off the night before:

> Sunday is spent in sleepy lounging about the fields, lying on the benches at home, when they have not slept off the Saturday night's debuach . . . anxiously waiting for the church leaving, when they rush to the house of the Red Lion.[8]

Drunkenness is probably the most consistent of the criticisms made about the nailers; and it would be naive to dismiss this aspect of their reputation out of hand. Irregular hours had something to do with it. Men, women and children laboured long periods until they almost dropped, then idled for a while. Many, once the wrought nails were delivered on Saturday, would do nothing until the following Tuesday. 'St Monday' was still going strong in Cradley Heath in the 1930s. But this approach was certainly not peculiar to nailmaking; it was just as true of some other trades and it was a long tradition, not just born of the last century. Daniel Defoe, having travelled around the country in the early decades of the eighteenth century, came to the conclusion that the English 'are the most lazy-diligent nation in the world'.

Levett Nokes, the man who thought long and hard about the plight of the nailers, wrote his little book *The Mysteries of the Wrought Nail Trade Revealed* just over 100 years ago in the hope that this would instigate the reforms he felt were necessary. In it he claimed drunkenness was interfering with the work of some nailers and at the same time tarring the rest with the same brush. He tells the story of a group of seven men (six married) who were 'out on the fly' in Bromsgrove and ended up selling the shoes off their feet (and the single man his socks!) to 'make up the last jug'.

There can be little doubt that some drunkenness did exist and not only among Worcestershire nailers. In the late eighteenth century and throughout most of the nineteenth excessive drink was a national problem among Englishmen of all classes. Two of Cruickshank's prints, 'The Bottle' and 'The Drunkard's Children', were circulated by the tens of thousands and every town came to have its temperance societies. But to some of the nailers at least the tippling shop proved a highly attractive alternative to the drudgery of the nailblock.

Who would really blame them, a bit of money in the pocket, if they went for a Saturday night spree to drown their sorrows in a little of the 'oh be joyful'? The pub was the hub of social life for the average Bromsgrovian— and there was quite a choice. In 1840 there were at least 59 inns, taverns and beerhouses in the town;[9] and for a population of less than 10,000 'a testimony to the flourishing coaching trade, lax licensing laws and not least to the town's nailers, toiling over their hot forges'.[10] In Belbroughton during this period there were four and sometimes five pubs; Catshill also had four and sometimes five; and in Bournheath there were two and later three pubs. In 'temperate' Sidemoor there was but a single alehouse.

It would have been very surprizing if nailers hadn't been good customers of the innkeepers bearing in mind the need, the opportunity and the temptation to drink. Nailing was after all one of the sweating trades and nailmakers had of necessity to drink ample fluids. The choice of a drinking-

A nailers' pub: the Horn and Trumpet (Kidderminster Road), now Clifford Cottage

hole was wide, in most instances on the doorstep, and there was very little else, especially in the town, to claim the attention of this large body of workers. Even some who had no intention of drinking must sometimes have been helped on their way by the fogger who deliberately made the

nailers wait about in his *wobble shop* for the iron rod in order to make sure
that any remaining bit of money was drunk up. The fogger thus reaped
large profits, 'and did an infinite deal of mischief to the stomachs of the
nailers by reason of the quality of the beer he kept on tap'.[11]

For drunkenness the local magistrates imposed heavy fines, without
however appearing to make any impact.

> George Butler, nailer of Sidemoor, charged with being drunk
> on 10th August 1885. Defendant admitted the case and that
> he had been convicted 34 times of drunkenness.

He was fined 5/- and 8/- costs, more than a week's wages. But the magistrates
a couple of months earlier had demonstrated their impartiality for in June
at the same court Henry Banner, a Sidemoor nailer, was fined 2/6 and 8/-
costs for being drunk at the Horn and Trumpet, Jabez Lammas, another
Sidemoor nailer, fined 2/6 and 1/- costs (very light) for the same offence,
and—lo and behold—Daniel Johnson, landlord of the said Horn and
Trumpet (now Clifford Cottage in Kidderminster Road) was fined £3 and
costs for 'permitting drunkenness on the premises'.[12]

Perhaps the pub provided a safety valve. In the early decades of this century
an annual event occurred which was as regular as Fair Day. A group of nailers
would save up by working late—very late—and when the kitty was ample
would give a few shillings to their wives and wend their way to an agreed
pub. There they would get blind drunk, sleeping where they could, until
the money ran out. They would return home and the next day trudge back
into the workshop to resume the monotonous round. Wives on the whole
understood this. But what was *their* escape valve? Only death according
to my grandmother!

Not everyone in any case supported the picture of the drunken nailer:

> Look at the nail-makers of Bromsgrove, who are the worst
> paid of all white slaves. I never heard of a single instance
> of a man's 'going on the beer' during all the days I spent
> in that picturesque but wicked little town.[13]

The Rev James Kidd of Catshill concluded a letter to the Inspectorate
of Factories (about the particularly sad case of a boy nailer) by declaring
drunken parents to be few, at least in Catshill;[14] and it is interesting to
speculate where the time and money could have come from to enable nailers

to get drunk as often as has been claimed (though parsley wine, a home-made brew popular among nailers, was very cheap to make). On 11 February 1911 the editor of the Bromsgrove Messenger was able to write (hand on heart?)

Bromsgrove is generally regarded as a sober town.*

The luckier nailers in the villages always had something other than nails, their good-sized gardens, a stark and pleasurable contrast to the nailshop. Gardens offered an immediate and healthy hobby; an extra source of support; an opportunity to take part in the growing number of produce shows which became an annual feature in chapel, pub and club; and eventually a way out of nailing into market gardening.

A number of nailers, including those in the town, kept pigeons, still a popular hobby in the district. Every little area had its club and the care and attention lavished on the feathered creatures was greater in some instances than that received by wives and children. Local pigeon fanciers have had a string of outstanding successes over the years and Bordeaux Billy is almost as well known to some locals as Socco Waldren, Billy Turner and Laddie Harris (the latter three, for the uninitiated, footballers, the first a pigeon).

In 1885 a new and permanent source of entertainment arrived to brighten the lives of the hard-up nailers. Bromsgrove Rovers got off to a stuttering start, playing in a field along Well Lane. But even for practice matches at the beginning of the season the club was drawing 2000 spectators whilst home league and cup games were watched by upward of 4000 (though many of these got in free simply by hopping over the hedge).

For the vast majority of nineteenth-century nailers the quality of life was poor in the extreme, without colour, without variety, choked by poverty and lack of opportunity. A few good times, some merry moments and the occasional bit of excitement there undoubtedly were. But only with the enforcement of school attendance and the creation of new employment opportunities did the lives of nailing families begin to change; and by that time there weren't many left.

* 'Tell that to the marines' has invariably been the response of old Bromsgrovians when acquainted with this bit of historical information.

Nine   Nailtalk

There are no nailers left in the area to talk to now; and no more than a handful of the children of nailers, two of whom appear below. There are still some around who remember seeing their grandparents (or great aunts and uncles) in their nailshops, but when that generation has gone every last memory of the great staple trade will have gone too.

IVY ELVINS is the daughter of Bromsgrove's last nailmaker and nailmaster, Charlie Troth. She recently returned to Bromsgrove and now lives in Broad Street, just round the corner from York Road in Sidemoor where she was born. At 82 years of age she can remember vividly her childhood in York Road and her dad's nailshops.

There were three cottages together at the top of York Road, all occupied by different members of the Troth family—one by Harold, one by grandma and grandad (later by uncle David), and the third by Dad and Mom. Dad's first nailshop was at the side of the house and you went up the back to the orchard belonging to Southalls at the farm. There was a lovely little stream which ran through the orchard, then disappeared under the road and came up the back of The Common, now called Broad Street, of course. This stream, I believe, came from the Washingstocks, the brook that ran past Barnsley Hall and on to Fockbury. But it's gone now, a great tragedy, really, because it was so beautiful. There was a well in our yard and the water was icy cold. Dad would drink gallons of this water every day—all nailers were permanently parched because of the hard work and the dust and the long hours.

Dad's first nailshop had three windows, all with wooden shutters on the outside. The fire and chimney were in the middle of the shop, and as you entered the first thing you saw was the scales on the table. This was where Dad weighed the nails brought in by the nailers working for him. Among his nailers were Liz and Edwin Rea of Holly Road, Grandad Joe Hodgkiss and Snaggy Porter.

Snaggy didn't always work for Dad; sometimes he went to Mason's or Roper's. But in the very hard times Dad would still give out iron and pay for the nails, keeping them at the back of the workshop. You had to go round the bench very carefully to get to the little space at the back where he stored the nails. He also kept them in the coal-house during slack periods, paying his nailers just the same. I don't know how he calculated the money because the system was so complicated and he wasn't a good reckoner. Mom was different, she was clever. She sewed up all the nailbags when they were full. This wasn't easy because the bags were lined with brown paper to stop the points or tangs from sticking out through the bags.

Dad bought his iron from Digbeth. Mom and I would order it and the big dealers would send a lorry round and have the nails taken to the station. Dad was a very good nailer. He made brush nails, clinkers, tenterhooks and many other types. We used to watch the different colours in the fire which changed as the bellows were pumped. The nails finished up a lovely deep violet colour which they said was because of the breeze he used. Dad wore a leather apron to stop the sparks burning him. And he always wore a flannelette vest which Mother used to make. She worked at Whitfields, the clothing factory, and was a good seamstress. She used to make up a shirt at a penny a time for local people.

Later on my Dad moved to his second nailshop up the garden. He made the big shed and there was much more room in it. My brother Ran, who worked for Bryant's as a mechanic, changed his job and made nails for Dad, both working together. Ran's heart wasn't really in nailing though and he moved to greener pastures at the Austin Motor Company. So Dad was on his own again.

Towards the end of my Dad's working life Mom would make a pot of tea and they would sit together on an orange box which they kept in the nailshop. They would look up the garden, drinking their tea and feeding the birds.

My father was a kind and generous man, loved and respected by all those who knew him.

LES GILES is an old sportsman of 84 years of age, an amateur who played for Bromsgrove Rovers and was given trials by professional clubs. He was good enough to have earned his living at both football and boxing if he had wanted to. But he'd no desire to be a professional sportsman.

The son of nailing parents, Les remembers distinctly one of the last of the old-fashioned nailmasters, William Mason, because of his imposing features, particularly his mutton-chop whiskers, and his white ear trumpet. Les used to deliver nails to the Mason warehouse in the High Street which was at the back of the International Stores.

There was a crock basin on a table at the bottom of the stairs, with three half-crowns in it. Mr Mason would always come down with you after weighing the nails upstairs and surreptitiously glance in the basin to see if any of the half-crowns were missing.

While Les's mother was an excellent nailer, he particularly remembers the prodigious feats of Snappy Troth who could make six nails from one heat! He remembers Charlie Troth too, but better still Charlie's dad David.

One day David Troth drew me to one side and emptied a chamois leather bag into his hand. 'Keep off the beer and cigarettes and you will be able to save some of these! I stared at the heap of golden sovereigns.'

With a glint in his eye Les likes to recall some of the old nailers, the likes of Zach Ashfield, Snaggy Porter and Nutshell Lammas of Melbourne Road, of Ash and Polly Giles, Mush Weaver, Billy Rea and Bull Brumfill (Broomfield), all of the Square in Providence Road in Sidemoor. And they all worked just that bit differently from each other.

One morning very early, about four o'clock, my father, Sid Giles, took me outside and said: 'Now just listen Leslie.' There was a click, click, thump and he said, 'That's Billy Rea.' Then another started up, then another, and by the time five o'clock came round all Sidemoor was at work. My father could tell by the sound of the hammer and then the banging of the oliver exactly which nailmaker it was. Bill Juggins's dad was unmistakable. He had an oliver weighing 56lbs—the heaviest in the whole of the Bromsgrove district.

(It is only a pity that Les Giles could not be persuaded to record more of his memories of the nail trade. Sadly he died a few weeks after the above conversation took place.)

ETHEL PARSONS was born in 1900 in Billy Street, Catshill. Her father was Laddie Harris, star of Bromsgrove Rovers from 1904—1912 before moving to Redditch and finally to Kidderminster. Mrs Parsons' grandfather was Nerky Harris, a nailmaker also of Billy Street, who would not allow any of his children into the nailshop ('a crime to teach a lad'). But grandma Harris, also a nailer, got her granddaughter to blow the bellows for her!

At nearly 90 years of age Mrs Parsons recalls some of the nailing characters who lived in and around Billy Street when she was a child.

At the bottom of Billy Street in the old cottage lived Tommy Bott and before him a man called Jelfs who had a horse and cart. Coming up Billy Street were rows of cottages at right angles off it and some alongside it. In the first row there was

> *Sam Deakin, nailer*
> *Roger Stokes, who cleaned the school*
> *Hannah and Eps Rea, both nailers*

In the second row

> *Reynolds family, nailers*
> *Johnny James, nailer*
> *Inky Field, nailer*

In the top row

> *The Allbutts, a lovely family with six children. The Allbutts were nailers. Mr Allbutt was killed in the 1914—18 War. Their great-granddaughter Gillian played netball for England.*
> *Bumper Collins, a huckster who worked the market with his horse and trap*
> *Wicked Wil Field, nailer*

In the two cottages at the top were

> *Grandad Harris, nailer*
> *Billy Harris (Dad's cousin)*

Down the other side of the street lived

> *Ike Juggins, a big man, he was the toolmaker. You took your tools to him for repair or got him to make new ones*
> *Ashwell Juggins (Billy Chat), Ike's brother, a nailer.*

At the bottom of the street was a pub called The Vine. The proprietor, a man called Byng, was also a wheelwright. Opposite the Crown my aunt, Hannah Perks, made nails in a cottage which she rented for 2/- a week. The land opposite the Crown was owned by a farmer called Joe Burton but known as Slethermuck (an old word for someone of a slow and deliberate disposition).

Up the Stourbridge Road past the school lived
>*Tommy Hatton, nailer*
>*Black Sam Juggins, nailer (who became a baker)*
>*Mrs Ward, nailer*
>*A little slaughter house came next*
>*Mrs Stokes (Aunt Seranne), nailer*
>*Mr and Mrs Gwynne, nailers, who cleaned the chapel*

Round the church was The Laurels, a nail warehouse where Mr Parry was nailmaster and round 'The Canister' were
>*Henry Fisher*
>*Steven Goode*
>*Nellie Weaver, nailer, who used to walk into Bromsgrove every Saturday morning to a nailmaster with her nails in a little trolley*

Next was the village hall where we used to go for a halfpenny dinner. They were lovely, and after dinner, as you left, they gave you a piece of bread and jam. Opposite the Ivy Cottage lived George Allbutt, in one of the hive of nail cottages.

Up Golden Cross Lane were
>*John Wagstaff*
>*Frank Wagstaff, baker*

At the back of the bakehouse was Donkey Row—all nailers' cottages. William Emus, last nailmaker in the area, lived just down an alley off Golden Cross Lane

Of all my memories the most vivid is as a small child hearing the clip-clop of a man from Fairfield early every morning as he walked to work at the Wagon Works in Aston Fields. You could set your clock by him.

SID TROTH lives in York Road in Sidemoor.

I was born in 1911 in Penny Pot Cottage at the top of Rocky Lane. It was a lovely nailmaker's cottage and we were happy there. However, it was put up for sale and as we were only tenants we had to get out. Jack Cuckoo bought it for £90 and we moved to Catshill, opposite the Ivy Cottage. Our cottage was one of a few owned by Catherine Manning who lived in the Strand in Bromsgrove, next to Petford's Lodging House. Mrs Manning was a big woman who would walk to Catshill on rent day to collect her rents. She was always wheeled back to Bromsgrove in a trolley, too well oiled to walk.

My parents weren't nailmakers but everyone else I knew in my childhood made nails for a living. I used to watch Lighty Wilkes next door to the Ivy Cottage. Lighty was a little man with a bent back, acquired from bending over the fire and the nailblock. There were two blocks in Lighty's shop and Mrs Lighty (we never called her anything else) made nails at the other block. They worked every day until it was way past dark—except Sunday. Mrs Lighty would on rare occasions knock off work and trot next door to the Ivy Cottage for half a bitter. But she drank it in seconds and was back at work almost immediately. The Lightys lived in Biddy Manning's Yard. Biddy was the rag and bone man who owned the three cottages in his yard. One day Biddy gave me a penny for a rabbit skin. I thought I was a millionaire. But my happiest memory of all is of the Liberal Club (later the village hall), opened by the Gibbins family of Barnt Green. I 'signed the pledge' there when I was about four years old! The Band of Hope was formed by Mrs Gibbins and it publicised the evils of drink (the alcoholic kind). For a halfpenny we were given a dinner and a piece of bread and jam as we left.

The Sunday School treat was held once a year and organized by the Baptists. We all went off in Mac Pinfield's wagon to the Beehive Farm and had races and games all afternoon. I remember we had to wear our tin mug round our necks tied to a piece of string in case we lost it. At home in our one-bedroom cottage there were ten of us altogether (eight children). I don't remember now how we slept but we had a large landing at the top of the stairs, so it was really like having two bedrooms. I remember a man called Shuker coming every Friday from Halesown to sell fish. My Mom would get two shovelfuls of sprats for threepence. At Billy Rush's fish and chip shop you could get as many chips as the family could eat for a halfpenny. Everyone enjoyed Fridays.

I don't remember *Wil Emus* but I remember clearly *Walter Kings* who was not only a good nailmaker but a preacher as well. His brother *Tubin* lost a leg in the First World War but he was as good on his crutch as most young men were on two legs.

I suppose one of the things I remember best from that time is having to walk from our cottage after school to my grandmother's house at the bottom of *Brimstone Lane* in *Worms Ash*. It was a long walk but we didn't mind it. When we got there we had to get the water for grandmother from a spring in the woods, carrying it in two buckets on a yoke over the shoulders.

Sid Troth outside the nailer's cottage where he was born

Epilogue

My sledge and hammer lie reclined
My bellows too have lost their wind
My fire's extinct, my forge decayed
And in my dust my vice is layed
My coal is spent, my iron is gone
My nails are drove, my work is done

Anon

Appendix A

A little nailing dictionary

Some of the words listed below are by no means peculiar to nailing; but they are useful to know in the context of this book.

Bate abatement, reduction in price
Bellas or 'bellasis', bellows
Bibble stone used for weighing
Bist are ('How bist?' 'How are you?')
Blartin' crying
Block wooden framework in which the jack and other tools were put
Bloom large block of iron weighing 30—40 lbs
Bore tool into which the partly finished nail was placed prior to heading
Breeze or 'gleeds', small pieces of coke
Breviting messing about
Bruhus brewhouse, usually the wash house
Chimmuk chimney (or 'chimbley')
Clane clean
Clemmed or 'clammed', hungry
Dunnock hedge sparrow
Fayther father
Fittle or 'fickle', food (from victuals)
Flays fleas
Fogger middleman (perhaps from 'petty-fogger', inferior and unscrupulous lawyer)
Gob mouth
Granch grind (as in teeth)
Hardy fixed chisel which partly severed the nail

Jack large block with holes into which various tools were fixed at different stages
Jummucksed 'all jummucksed up', all mixed up
Ketch or 'kitch', catch
Larrup to beat
Mawken fool or idiot. ('Yowm talkin' like a mawken.')
Meck make
Miskin rubbish bin
Mother's ruin gin
Muffle fire
'No iron' no work
Oh be joyful alcoholic beverage, usually beer
Oliver large hammer for making large nails
Ommer hammer
Out on the fly out on a spree
Paddle lever tapped to eject completed nail
Pudding bag cul-de-sac
Rock staff handle pumped to work the bellows and provide draught for the fire
Scale skin formed on hot metal when worked

Steady small block set in the jack to fashion the point of the nail

Stint or 'stent', weight of nails due from rod iron

Swede basher Brummy name for anyone living in Bromsgrove

Tale thousand

Tang point of the nail

Teasers bellows

Tiswas pieces of nail bent to make four sharp points

Up country to Bromsgrovians any place north, especially the Black Country

Wairter water

Wassin gullet ('Get this down thee wassin')

Wick week

Wobble shop alehouse

Yawpin talking

Yoddin' making the head (yod) of the n a i l

In Bromsgrove, as up country, we 'spake as we dun'

Appendix B

Richard Juggins

In the last three decades of the nineteenth century Richard Juggins became the voice of the Black Country craftsmen, a role for which his industrial experience and personal qualities fitted him almost to perfection.

He was born in 1843 and began work in a nut and bolt workshop at the tender age of seven. Four years later his father, a miner, was killed in a pit accident. By 1870 he had formed the Nut and Bolt Makers' Association for which he acted as part-time secretary, a development his employers clearly didn't relish for a year later he was sacked from his job for agitating. This probably served only to sharpen his determination to get men and women to join together to better their conditions; and within seven years of losing his job he had organized the workers in the nut and bolt industry from Newcastle in the north to South Wales.

In the West Midlands wage bargaining, as far as skilled craftsmen were concerned, was becoming a question of list prices for finished jobs. This had always been the case in the nail trade and other domestic industries and Richard Juggins worked for this approach to be applied to the nut and bolt industry. In 1877, when the employers proposed a reduction in wages, an independent arbitrator was appointed—no less a man than Joseph Chamberlain who, when he became President of the Board of Trade, was succeeded by his brother Richard. In 1885 the first Nut and Bolt Wages Board for South Staffordshire was formed.

As the only professional trade union organizer in the Black Country Richard Juggins was especially keen to get unions working together and was instrumental in forming the Midland Counties' Trades Federation. In 1887 the chainmakers asked him to organize their strike which he did with huge success; and four years later he organized the last great strike of Bromsgrove nailers along the same lines, soliciting the support, both moral and practical, of a wide range of organizations and individuals.

Richard Juggins was a Methodist lay preacher and became a lifelong

Liberal. He could, had he wished, have entered the national political field but he chose instead to work in local politics. In 1895 when he died there was still only a tiny minority of the working population in union membership—11% in Northumberland and Durham but less than 5% in the West Midlands. But perhaps it is true, as some have argued, that though there may have been fewer unionists then there was more unionism.

An outstanding figure in Midlands industrial life, Richard Juggins earned his reputation for honesty, high standards, and a vigorous approach to his work, qualities that were combined with natural humility. He was, according to an obituary in the London Morning Leader of 6 March 1895, a 'natural orator' and 'an excellent organizer' who conducted Midlands strikes 'in a singularly practical manner'. He was certainly both loved and respected in the Bromsgrove area where his favourite way of summing up the aim of all strikes became well known: 'Peace with honour'.

Eliza Tinsley—the 'Black Widow'

The great nailmistress of the Black Country was born in 1813, the daughter of Benjamin Butler, a maltster who later kept the Golden Fleece, a public house in Wolverhampton. At twenty-six Eliza married Thomas Tinsley, a Sedgley nailmonger, and went to live in Dudley Road, Sedgley. Thomas died in 1851; so after only twelve years of marriage Eliza was left with five children (the sixth and eldest also died in 1851) and a business on her hands. To everyone's surprise Eliza, donned in the black that widowhood then demanded, proceeded to take over her husband's business as well as bring up her children. She ran the firm for twenty-one years, until she was not far short of sixty, all the time expanding the business throughout the Black Country and its fringes, travelling far and wide to further its development against great competition. Eventually the firm of Eliza Tinsley and Co became the largest nailmasters in Staffordshire with warehouses in Bromsgrove, Catshill, Dudley, Old Hill, Sedgley, Stourbridge and Wolverhampton. It was prominent in the Nailmasters' Association which met from the late eighteenth century onwards to agree prices for all types and sizes of nails; and when Mrs Tinsley sold out to a partnership in 1872 the new firm continued to trade under her name.

It was a wise decision, for Eliza Tinsley's reputation was for fair dealing among both business associates and the nailmakers she employed. She died in 1882 at The Limes in Sedgley, having employed at one time more than 4000 people. The name of this able and energetic businesswoman, however, lives on, for a century after her death the Eliza Tinsley Group is a familiar element in the industrial make-up of the West Midlands.

'No iron' (from 'The White Slaves of England, *Pearson's Magazine,* 1896)

Appendix C

Bromsgrove nailers' surnames in 1840

Many of the surnames common among nailers 150 years ago are still prominent in the area today. The following is a list of all the nailing surnames to be found in Bentley's History and Directory of Bromsgrove, rearranged in order of popularity. The first figure shows the number of nailers listed with a particular surname; the bracketed figure shows the number of all those listed in Bromsgrove bearing that same surname. Both figures refer to heads of families rather than individuals.

Banner	19	(20)	Hughes	4	(9)	Carpenter	2	(2)
Giles	15	(15)	Ince	4	(4)	Chandler	2	(3)
Crawford	12	(12)	Lewis	4	(6)	Chinn	2	(2)
Smith	12	(23)	Perry	4	(4)	Clark	2	(2)
Harris	10	(10)	Pinfield	4	(5)	Crane	2	(4)
Jones	10	(16)	Stanton	4	(4)	Duffill	2	(4)
Juggins	10	(13)	Warman	4	(4)	Dyer	2	(2)
Liddell	9	(9)	Yeates	4	(6)	Gower	2	(2)
Johnson	8	(12)	Albutt	3	(3)	Hill	2	(6)
Walters	8	(9)	Barrow	3	(3)	Hodgetts	2	(2)
James	7	(7)	Cottril	3	(3)	Horton	2	(5)
Eades	6	(6)	Hall	3	(5)	Lacy	2	(4)
Kimberley	6	(7)	Manning	3	(4)	Laugher	2	(3)
King(s)	6	(11)	Phillips	3	(3)	Sanders	2	(10)
Powell	6	(8)	Taylor	3	(5)	Waldron	2	(3)
Wakeman	6	(7)	Troth	3	(4)	Brooks	1	(3)
Amos	5	(5)	Ward	3	(7)	Cox	1	(3)
Bing	5	(5)	Webley	3	(4)	Halfpenny	1	(2)
Wardle	5	(5)	White	3	(6)	Knight	1	(4)
Wheeler	5	(7)	Wilkes	3	(3)	Noakes	1	(3)
Wilson	5	(7)	(H)ancox	2	(2)	Perks	1	(1)
Bratt	4	(4)	Ashfield	2	(3)	Porter	1	(3)
Brighton	4	(6)	Bellamy	2	(3)	Tilt	1	(1)
Edwards	4	(7)	Broomfield	2	(2)	Whitehouse	1	(5)
Fisher	4	(6)	Butler	2	(4)			

Appendix D

I Nailmakers in Bromsgrove as a percentage of the population.

Year	Population	No. of nailmakers	% of population
1781	4,650*	900*	19
1831	8,612	1,169	14
1841	9,676	3,042	31
1851	10,310	3,119	30
1861	10,823	2,514	23
1871	11,791	2,561	22
1881	12,801	No figures available	
1891	13,006	1,500	12
1901	14,106	964	7
1911	16,138	1,069	7
1921	No census returns		
1931	38,496		
1941	No census returns		
1951	52,412	5	0.0001

* John Lacey's estimated figures
1831 onwards: population figures from the censuses; number of nailmakers from the trade directories
1931 onwards: population figures are for the urban and rural districts of Bromsgrove combined

II Nailmakers in Worcestershire as a percentage of the national nailmaking population.

	Male nailmakers				Female nailmakers		
Year	England & Wales	Worcestershire	% of total	Year	England & Wales	Worcestershire	% of total
1841	13,902	3,905	28	1841	4,039	2,321	57.5
1851	16,965	5,150	30	1851	9,075	5,150	57
1861	15,369	5,040	33	1861	10,761	4,224	39
1871	12,367	4,211	34	1871	10,874	4,608	42
1881	9,584	3,613	38	1881	9,138	3,926	42
1891	5,127	2,012	39	1891	4,816	2,140	45
1901	3,163	1,140	36	1901	2,604	1,254	48
1911	2,925	1,069	37	1911	1,685	698	41

From: 1841—1911 censuses

The 1911 census was the last one to include nailmaking as a separate occupational category.

Appendix E

1. The will of Martyne Blicke

Below is an extract from the inventory of goods owned by Martyne Blicke of Bromsgrove at the time of his death. Blicke was a small-scale farmer as well as a nailer, keeping cattle, sheep, pigs, poultry and three hives of bees. For Blicke's will to be proved a group of reputable and competent neighbours had to 'appraise' all his belongings and this is what John Carpenter, Henry Cookes, John Knight, Willud Chance and Henry Dugard did on 31 July in 1611. They noted and evaluated the goods in each room – the cellars over the hall and over the chamber, the main chamber itself, the hall and the buttery – and all his livestock and 'implements of husbandry' outside. In between these two areas they listed what was in the nailshop.

In the Shopp

Item   a paire of bellowes   XX^s
Item   iiii studyes   iv hammers   vi
bores   iii paire of tongues,   iii paire   vii^s
of Clores   ii fire shovels,   ii files
wight of Iron p(ri)sed at

Appendix E

2. The will of Thomas Liddell

I Thomas Liddell of Warbridge Lane in the Parish of Bromsgrove in the County of Worcester Nailer being of sensible and disposing mind —

memory and understanding, for which I desire to be thankful, to — ... — Almighty God Do make this my last will and testament in manner following / that is to say / I give and devise all those my three Cottages — ... — Tenements or Dwellinghouses with their Shop, Gardens and other ... —

outbuildings thereunto belonging Also all those my three several Plecks of Meadow Ground adjoining or near adjoining thereto situate and — being at Warbridge Lane in the Parish of Bromsgrove in the County of Worcester aforesaid and now in my own possession and my Tenants

Daniel Liddell, and Isaac Rutter Unto Thomas Ledbeter of Burnheath, and William Liddell of Catshill both in the said Parish of Bromsgrove Nailers and to their heirs executors administrators and assigns for —

Extract from the will of Thomas Liddell, nailer, made in 1819

Notes

A great variety of both original and secondary sources, as well as people, were consulted in the preparation of this book. Some are mentioned in the text, others are detailed below.

Several have been quoted on a number of occasions and for simplification will be referred to as follows:

Court   W H B Court, *The Rise of the Midland Industries 1600—1838*, 2nd ed., 1953
Davies   E I Davies, *The Midland Hand-Wrought Nail Trade* (unpublished thesis held at Birmingham University)
The Messenger   The Bromsgrove and Droitwich Weekly Messenger
Nokes   Levett Nokes, *The Mysteries of the Wrought Nail Trade Revealed* (1884)
Palmer   *Palmer's Bromsgrove Almanack and Directory*
Sherard   Robert Sherard, 'The White Slaves of England', *Pearson's Magazine* (1896)
Sweating   *Third Report of the Select Committee on Sweating* (1888)

Chapter One

1   John Cotton's 'Nails Old and New' can be found in *Chimes and Rhymes* (1903)
2   For a reassessment of the finds see 'The Late Iron Age Metalworks from Bulbury, Dorset' by Barrie Cunliffe in *Antiquaries' Journal LII* (1972)
3   William Hutton, *History of Birmingham*, 6th ed., (1835)
4   *Victoria County History* Vol 2
5   John Leland, *The Itinerary of John Leland*, ed. L Toulmin Smith (1908)
6   *Victoria County History* Vol 2 p 272
7   See *Newcomen Society Transactions* Vol 8 p 104
8   Historical MSS Commission's Report III (2), quoted in *Victoria County History*
9   Court
10 T R Nash, *Collections for the History of Worcestershire*, 2nd ed., (1799)

11   In *The Story of Bromsgrove* William G Leadbetter suggests that nailmaking was introduced into the area by Huguenot refugees in either the late sixteenth or late seventeenth century. The origin of the Bromsgrove trade would appear to be much more natural in view of the proximity of the raw materials
12   From the Cotton Collection in Birmingham University
13   John Cotton, *Chimes and Rhymes*
14   Court
15   Thomas Newcomen of Dartford had close links with Bromsgrove. He must often have stayed here on his way from his home to the West Midlands, being named as a trustee of the Baptist Church's first meeting house. He himself combined successful engineering with lay preaching
16   Rhys Jenkins, 'Links in the History of Engineering—the Slitting Mill', *Engineer*, 24 May and 7 June 1918
17   *Ibid*
18   T R Nash, *Collections for the History of Worcestershire*, 2nd ed., (1799)
19   To be found in the apprenticeship records held in Worcestershire County Record Office
20   Court
21   Davies
22   From the Bolton Papers, quoted in Court
23   *Ibid*
24   Hutton, *History of Birmingham*, 6th ed., (1835)
25   John Lacey, *Queries Proposed for Promoting a Parochial History of Great Britain Originally Proposed by the Society of Antiquaries in London—Bromsgrove parish, Worcestershire 1778* (MSS in the Cotton Collection)
26   1841 census
27   Though not quite as many as 10,000,000 a day or 50,000,000 a week since Mr Palmer's 'guesstimate' of 4000 nailers was inaccurate: the following year's census showed the number had already dropped to 2514. It had peaked 10 years earlier
28   Palmer
29   Davies

Chapter Two

1   Sherard
2   Berrow's Worcester Jornal, 7 November 1793
3   *Ibid*
4   See page 26
5   *Truck Commission Report* (1871)
6   *Pigot's Directory of Worcestershire*
7   See, for example, *Bentley's History and Directory of Bromsgrove* (1840)
8   Palmer, 1899
9   Palmer, 1870
10   *Billing's Directory and Gazeteer of the County of Worcester* (1855)
11   Palmer, 1865
12   *Littlebury's Directory and Gazeteer of Worcester and District* (1879)
13   Palmer, 1865
14   *Littlebury's Directory and Gazeteer of Worcester and District* (1879)
15   Dr George Fletcher, 'Reminiscences and Recollections' published in the Messenger between 28 December 1929 and 1 September 1930
16   *Ibid*
17   *Billing's Directory and Gazeteer of the County of Worcester* (1855)
18   The Messenger, 26 April 1936

19   Privately owned and in excellent condition

Chapter Three

1   Sherard
2   Nokes
3   William G Leadbetter, *The Story of Bromsgrove* (1946)
4   Bromsgrove Court Rolls, quoted by A F C Burrows, *Worcestershire Historical Society*
5   *English Historical Review*, Vol XXXI
6   Nokes
7   House of Commons Select Committee 1812
8   *Report of the Chief Inspector of Factories and Workshops* (1879)
9   Nokes

Chapter Four

1   *The Life of William Hutton* (1816)
2   From the Bolton Papers, quoted in Court
3   Sweating
4   *Ibid*
5   *Ibid*
6   Factory Inspectors' Report for 1872
7   Davies
8   Nokes
9   Elihu Burritt, *Walks in the Black Country and its Green Borderland* (1868)

Chapter Five

1   Elihu Burritt, *Walks in the Black Country and its Green Borderland* (1868)
2   Sherard
3   *Ibid*
4   W A Cotton, *Facts and Notes about Nailmakers and Nailmaking* (1884)
5   Sweating
6   Sherard
7   *Ibid*

Chapter Six

1   Census of Production
2   Nokes
3   A Bromsgrove nailmaster quoted in the Birmingham Daily Post, 25 June 1863
4   Nokes
5   Held in the Worcestershire County Record Office
6   Report of the 1837 Nailmasters' Association meetings, quoted in Samuel Timmins, *Birmingham and the Midland Hardware District* (1866)

Karl Henn, *The Hand-made Nail Trade of Dudley and District* (unpublished thesis)
8   Nokes
9   1 June 1843
10 Birmingham Daily Post, 25 June 1863
11 Nokes
12 No Kings can ever again walk head in air down the High Street!
13 The Messenger, 28 June 1862
14 The Messenger, 26 July 1862
15 *Ibid*
16 The Messenger, 2 August 1862
17 The Messenger, 15 July 1863
18 See page 28
19 The Messenger, 6 June 1863
20 The Messenger, 9 January 1869
21 The Messenger, 20 February 1869
22 The Messenger, 27 February 1869
23 The Messenger, 5 June 1869
24 The Messenger, 11 September 1869
25 The Messenger, 31 August 1875
26 The Messenger, 18 May 1878
27 The Messenger, 17 September 1887
28 The Messenger, 29 October 1887
29 The Messenger, 2 April 1887

Chapter Seven

1   The Messenger, 4 April 1891
2   *Report of the Royal Commission on Labour* (1892)
3   Davies

Chapter Eight

1   Rev Arthur Wilkes, *Our chapel* (1931)
2   Jennifer Heaton, *The Story of Methodism*, quoted in A B Crane, *The Sidemoor Saga* (1970)
3   A B Crane, *The Sidemoor Saga* (1970)
4   *Ibid*
5   Rev Arthur Wilkes, *Our Chapel* (1931)
6   Factory Inspectors' Report, 31 October 1868
7   Sherard
8   This accusation came from a doctor quoted in the Factory Inspectors' Report of 31 October 1868
9   *Bentley's History and Directory of Bromsgrove* (1840)
10 Alan and Sheila Richards, *Bromsgrove Now and Then* (1988)
11 W A Cotton, *Facts and Notes about Nailmakers and Nailmaking* (1884)
12 The Messenger, 22 June 1885
13 Sherard
14 Factory Inspectors' Report of November 1872

Index